THE
BUSINESSWOMAN'S
TOPICAL BIBLE

NEW I̶̶̶̶̶̶̶̶̶̶̶̶̶̶̶̶NAL

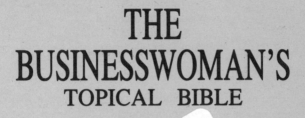

Tulsa, Oklahoma

Presented By:
Wisdom International
P. O. Box 747
Dallas, Texas 75221
214/518-1833

Published by
Honor Books
P. O. Box 55388
Tulsa, Oklahoma 74155

2nd Printing
Over 25,000 in Print

The Businesswoman's Topical Bible
All rights reserved.
No reproduction of this work
may be made without prior written
permission of the publisher.

All Scripture references are from
The Holy Bible, New International Version.
Copyright © 1973, 1978, 1984
by the International Bible Society.
Used by permission of Zondervan Bible Publishers.

ISBN 1-56292-029-4

Presented
to

_____

by

_____

_____

Date

Contents

The Salvation Experience
Your Relationship With God

Your Prayer Life 15

Your Study of God's Word........................... 18

Your Attitude Toward Praise and Worship 22

Your Hourly Obedience to God..................... 26

Your Attitude

The Businesswoman and Faith 31

The Businesswoman and Wisdom 35

The Businesswoman and Strength 39

The Businesswoman and Peace of Mind 43

The Businesswoman and Integrity 46

The Businesswoman and Commitment 49

The Businesswoman and Ambition................. 52

The Businesswoman and Leadership............... 55

The Businesswoman and Respect................... 56

The Businesswoman and a Servant's Heart....... 58

The Businesswoman and Honesty 62

The Businesswoman and an Achiever's Attitude. 64

The Businesswoman and Diligence................. 66

The Businesswoman and Loyalty 69

The Businesswoman and Decisiveness............. 71

The Businesswoman and Negotiation 74

The Businesswoman and Goal-Setting 76

The Businesswoman and Motivation............... 79

The Businesswoman and New Ideas 84

The Businesswoman and Wise Counsel 88

Your Work

When a Customer Is Dissatisfied 93

When a Customer Berates or Offends You 95

When a Customer Does Not Pay His Bills 98

When a Customer Becomes a Nuisance 100

When a Customer Is Dishonest 102

When a Customer Embarrasses You 104

When Your Employee Disappoints You...........107

When Your Employee Cheats You..................109

When Your Employee Makes a Costly Error 112

When Your Employee Slanders You...............113

When Your Employee Is Hurting 118

When Your Employee Has a Personal Crisis 120

When Your Employee Needs Motivation
  or Incentive 123

When Your Employee Faces Termination 127

When You Lose a Key Employee 130

When Your Partnership Is Threatened.............132

When Your Colleague Needs Your Support......135

When You Are Deceived 137

When You Feel Betrayed 143

When You Are Jealous 147

When You Feel Used 150

When You Face Illegal or Unfair Competition ..153

When You Are Asked To Participate
  in Unscrupulous Business Activities 156

When Your Business Is Failing 158

When You Face Litigation............................161

When You Face a Hostile Board 164

When You Have Made a Costly Mistake 169

When Calamity Strikes 173

When the Success of Your Business
    Depends on You Alone 177

Your Daily Schedule

When You Feel Disorganized 181
When Your Schedule Is Overbooked 183
When Your Day Falls Apart 186
When You Face Constant Interruptions 190
When You Need a Break............................ 192

Your Family

When You Face Marital Problems 195
When Your Spouse Is Unsupportive 198
When a Family Member Faces Sickness 200
When Your Family Time Is Inadequate 202
When Your Work Schedule Interferes With
    Your Church Life 206

Your Finances

When It Seems Impossible To Pay Your Bills ... 211
When You Need a Financial or
    Marketing Plan....................................... 214
When You Face a Volatile Economy 218
When You Are Tempted To Cheat................. 221
When Tithing Seems Too Difficult................. 224
When a Business Deal Falls Through.............. 228

Your Personal Life

When You Are Overworked......................... 231
When You Are Under Stress 233
When You Feel Anxious 237

When You Face Controversy........................240
When You Feel Like Compromising 244
When You Feel Like Lashing Out 246
When You Feel Threatened.........................249
When You Feel Depressed...........................251
When You Feel Lonely...............................254
When You Feel Like Giving Up....................257
When You Need To Forgive 261
When You Need Comfort............................264
When You Need Encouragement 267
When You Need Faith................................271
When You Need Healing.............................275
When You Need Joy 279
When You Need Love 283
When You Need Patience 288
When You Need Peace 292
When You Need Protection.........................295
When You Need Self-Control 298
When You Need Strength............................302
When You Need Wisdom 304
When You Need Deliverance 308
When You Do Not Feel God's Presence..........311
When You Have Bad Memories of the Past......313
When People Think You Are Weird...............315
When You Do Not Feel Like God Hears You...315
When You Want To Be Close To God............318

The Salvation Experience

**There Are Three Basic Reasons
To Believe the Bible Is
the Infallible and Pure Word of God**

1. *No human would have written a standard this high*. Think of the best person you know. You must admit he would have left certain scriptures out had he written the Bible. So the Bible projects an inhuman standard and way of life. It has to be God because no man you know would have ever written a standard that high.

2. *There is an aura, a climate, a charisma, a presence the Bible generates which no other book in the world creates.* Lay an encyclopedia on your table at the restaurant, nobody will look at you twice. But when you lay your Bible on the table, they will stare at you, watch you chew your food, and even read your license plate when you get in your car! Why? The Bible creates the presence of God and forces a reaction in the hearts of men.

3. *The nature of man is changed when he reads the Bible.* Men change. *Peace* enters into their spirits. Joy wells up within their lives. Men like what they become when they read this book. Men accept Christ, because this Bible says Jesus Christ is the Son of God and that all have sinned and the wages of sin will bring death; and the only

forgiveness that they can find is through Jesus, the Son of God.

Three Basic Reasons
for Accepting Christ

1. *You needed forgiveness.* At some point in your life, you will want to be clean. You will hate guilt; you will crave purity. You have a built-in desire toward God, and you will have to address that appetite at some point in your life.

2. *You need a friend.* You may be sitting there saying, "But, don't I have friends?" Yes, but you have never had a friend like Jesus. Nobody can handle the information about your life as well as He can. He is the most consistent relationship you will ever know. Human friends vacillate in their reaction, depending on your mood or theirs. Jesus Christ never changes his opinion of you. Nobody can tell Him anything which will change His mind about you. You cannot enjoy His world without His companionship.

3. *You needed a future.* All men have a built-in need for immortality, a craving for an eternity. God placed it within us. D.L. Moody once made a statement, "One of these days you are going to hear that I'm dead and gone. When you do, don't believe a word of it. I'll be more alive then, than at any other time in my life." Each of us wonders about eternity. What is death like? What happens when I die? Is there a hell? a heaven? a God? a

devil? What happens? Every man wants to be around tomorrow. The only guarantee you will have of a future is to have the Eternal One on the inside of you. *He is Jesus Christ, the Son of God!*

The Gospel means Good News, you can change; your sins can be forgiven; your guilt can be dissolved; God loves *you!* He wants to be the difference in your life. All have sinned and come short of the glory of God." Romans 3:23. "The wages of sin is death." Romans 6:23. You might say, what does that mean? It means that all unconfessed sin will be judged and penalized, but that is not the end of the story. The second part of verse 23 says "but the gift of God is eternal life through Jesus Christ our Lord." What does that mean? It means that between the wrath and judgment of God upon your sin, Jesus Christ the Son of God stepped in and absorbed your judgment and your penalty for you. God says if you recognize and respect Him and His worth as the Son of God, judgment will be withheld, and you will receive a pardon, forgiveness of all your mistakes.

What do you have to do? "If you believe in your heart that Jesus is the Son of God and that God raised him from the dead on the third day, and confess that with your mouth, then you will be saved." Romans 10:9-10. What does the word "saved" mean? *Removed from danger.* It simply means if you respect and recognize the worth of Jesus Christ, God will take you out of the danger zone and receive you as a child of the Most High

God. What is His gift that you are to receive? His Son. "For God so loved the world that he gave his only begotten Son, that whosoever believeth in Him should not perish but have everlasting life." John 3:16. How do you accept His Son? Accept His mercy. How do you reject your sins? Confess them and turn away from them. "If I confess my sins he is faithful and just to forgive me my sins and to cleanse me from all unrighteousness." 1 John 1:9. That is the Gospel.

Your Relationship With God

Your Prayer Life

Look to the LORD and his strength; seek his face always.

1 Chronicles 16:11

If my people, who are called by my name, will humble themselves and pray and seek my face and turn from their wicked ways, then will I hear from heaven and will forgive their sin and will heal their land.

2 Chronicles 7:14

My heart says of you, "Seek his face!" Your face, LORD, I will seek.

Psalm 27:8

By day the LORD directs his love, at night his song is with me — a prayer to the God of my life.

Psalm 42:8

But I call to God, and the LORD saves me. Evening, morning and noon I cry out in distress, and he hears my voice.

Psalm 55:16,17

Glory in his holy name; let the hearts of those who seek the LORD rejoice.

Look to the LORD and his strength; seek his face always.

Psalm 105:3,4

In return for my friendship they accuse me, but I am a man of prayer.

Psalm 109:4

The LORD is near to all who call on him, to all who call on him in truth.

Psalm 145:18

Seek the LORD while he may be found; call on him while he is near.

Isaiah 55:6

If you believe, you will receive whatever you ask for in prayer.

Matthew 21:22

Watch and pray so that you will not fall into temptation. The spirit is willing, but the body is weak.

Matthew 26:41

Very early in the morning, while it was still dark, Jesus got up, left the house and went off to a solitary place, where he prayed.

Mark 1:35

Therefore I tell you, whatever you ask for in prayer, believe that you have received it, and it will be yours.

Mark 11:24

Be on guard! Be alert! You do not know when that time will come.

Mark 13:33

Then Jesus told his disciples a parable to show them that they should always pray and not give up.
Luke 18:1

Be always on the watch, and pray that you may be able to escape all that is about to happen, and that you may be able to stand before the Son of Man.

Luke 21:36

In the same way, the Spirit helps us in our weakness. We do not know what we ought to pray for, but the Spirit himself intercedes for us with groans that words cannot express.

Romans 8:26

Be joyful in hope, patient in affliction, faithful in prayer.

Romans 12:12

And pray in the Spirit on all occasions with all kinds of prayers and requests. With this in mind, be alert and always keep on praying for all the saints.

Ephesians 6:18

Pray continually.

1 Thessalonians 5:17

I want men everywhere to lift up holy hands in prayer, without anger or disputing.

1 Timothy 2:8

Let us then approach the throne of grace with confidence, so that we may receive mercy and find grace to help us in our time of need.

Hebrews 4:16

But you, dear friends, build yourselves up in your most holy faith and pray in the Holy Spirit.

Jude 1:20

Your Study of God's Word

These commandments that I give you today are to be upon your hearts.

Deuteronomy 6:6

The secret things belong to the LORD our God, but the things revealed belong to us and to our children forever, that we may follow all the words of this law.

Deuteronomy 29:29

No, the word is very near you; it is in your mouth and in your heart so you may obey it.

Deuteronomy 30:14

Do not let this Book of the Law depart from your mouth; meditate on it day and night, so that you may be careful to do everything written in it. Then you will be prosperous and successful.

Joshua 1:8

He remembers his covenant forever, the word he commanded, for a thousand generations.

1 Chronicles 16:15

Accept instruction from his mouth and lay up his words in your heart.

Job 22:22

I have not departed from the commands of his lips; I have treasured the words of his mouth more than my daily bread.

Job 23:12

Blessed is the man who does not walk in the counsel of the wicked or stand in the way of sinners or sit in the seat of mockers.
But his delight is in the law of the LORD, and on his law he meditates day and night.

Psalm 1:1,2

The law of the LORD is perfect, reviving the soul. The statutes of the LORD are trustworthy, making wise the simple.

Psalm 19:7

Since you are my rock and my fortress, for the sake of your name lead and guide me.

Psalm 31:3

I will instruct you and teach you in the way you should go; I will counsel you and watch over you.

Psalm 32:8

The law of his God is in his heart; his feet do not slip.

Psalm 37:31

How can a young man keep his way pure? By living according to your word.

I have hidden your word in my heart that I might not sin against you.

Your word is a lamp to my feet and a light for my path.

Psalm 119:9,11,105

When you walk, they will guide you; when you sleep, they will watch over you; when you awake, they will speak to you.

For these commands are a lamp, this teaching is a light, and the corrections of discipline are the way to life.

Proverbs 6:22,23

Commit to the LORD whatever you do, and your plans will succeed.

Proverbs 16:3

Whether you turn to the right or to the left, your ears will hear a voice behind you, saying, "This is the way; walk in it."

Isaiah 30:21

The grass withers and the flowers fall, but the word of our God stands forever.

Isaiah 40:8

Therefore everyone who hears these words of mine and puts them into practice is like a wise man who built his house on the rock.

Matthew 7:24

Jesus replied, "You are in error because you do not know the Scriptures or the power of God."

Matthew 22:29

Heaven and earth will pass away, but my words will never pass away.

Mark 13:31

You diligently study the Scriptures because you think that by them you possess eternal life. These are the Scriptures that testify about me.

John 5:39

To the Jews who had believed him, Jesus said, "If you hold to my teaching, you are really my disciples.
Then you will know the truth, and the truth will set you free."

John 8:31,32

Consequently, faith comes from hearing the message, and the message is heard through the word of Christ.

Romans 10:17

All Scripture is God-breathed and is useful for teaching, rebuking, correcting and training in righteousness, so that the man of God may be thoroughly equipped for every good work.

2 Timothy 3:16,17

Through these he has given us his very great and precious promises, so that through them you may participate in the divine nature and escape the corruption in the world caused by evil desires.

For prophecy never had its origin in the will of man, but men spoke from God as they were carried along by the Holy Spirit.

2 Peter 1:4,21

Your Attitude Toward Praise and Worship

I call to the LORD, who is worthy of praise, and I am saved from my enemies.

2 Samuel 22:4

Ascribe to the LORD the glory due his name. Bring an offering and come before him; worship the LORD in the splendor of his holiness.

1 Chronicles 16:29

With praise and thanksgiving they sang to the LORD: ''He is good; his love to Israel endures forever.'' And all the people gave a great shout of praise to the LORD, because the foundation of the house of the LORD was laid.

Ezra 3:11

But I, by your great mercy, will come into your house; in reverence will I bow down toward your holy temple.

Psalm 5:7

I will give you thanks in the great assembly; among throngs of people I will praise you.

Psalm 35:18

Blessed are those who dwell in your house; they are ever praising you. Selah.

Psalm 84:4

It is good to praise the LORD and make music to your name, O Most High, to proclaim your love in the morning and your faithfulness at night.

Psalm 92:1,2

Come, let us bow down in worship, let us kneel before the LORD our Maker.

Psalm 95:6

Shout for joy to the LORD, all the earth.

Worship the LORD with gladness; come before him with joyful songs.

Know that the LORD is God. It is he who made us, and we are his; we are his people, the sheep of his pasture.

Enter his gates with thanksgiving and his courts with praise; give thanks to him and praise his name.

Psalm 100:1-4

Let them give thanks to the LORD for his unfailing love and his wonderful deeds for men.
Let them exalt him in the assembly of the people and praise him in the council of the elders.

Psalm 107:8,32

I will bow down toward your holy temple and will praise your name for your love and your faithfulness, for you have exalted above all things your name and your word.

Psalm 138:2

Praise the LORD. Praise God in his sanctuary; praise him in his mighty heavens.
Praise him for his acts of power; praise him for his surpassing greatness.
Praise him with the sounding of the trumpet, praise him with the harp and lyre, praise him with tambourine and dancing, praise him with the strings and flute, praise him with the clash of cymbals, praise him with resounding cymbals.
Let everything that has breath praise the LORD. Praise the LORD.

Psalm 150:1-6

Sing for joy, O heavens, for the LORD has done this; shout aloud, O earth beneath. Burst into song, you mountains, you forests and all your trees, for the LORD has redeemed Jacob, he displays his glory in Israel.

Isaiah 44:23

Jesus said to him, "Away from me, Satan! For it is written: 'Worship the Lord your God, and serve him only.' "

Matthew 4:10

Jesus answered, "It is written: 'Worship the Lord your God and serve him only.' "

Luke 4:8

Yet a time is coming and has now come when the true worshipers will worship the Father in spirit and truth, for they are the kind of worshipers the Father seeks. God is spirit, and his worshipers must worship in spirit and in truth.

John 4:23,24

We know that God does not listen to sinners. He listens to the godly man who does his will.

John 9:31

So what shall I do? I will pray with my spirit, but I will also pray with my mind; I will sing with my spirit, but I will also sing with my mind.

1 Corinthians 14:15

For it is we who are the circumcision, we who worship by the Spirit of God, who glory in Christ Jesus, and who put no confidence in the flesh.

Philippians 3:3

Devote yourselves to prayer, being watchful and thankful.

Colossians 4:2

I want men everywhere to lift up holy hands in prayer, without anger or disputing.

1 Timothy 2:8

You also, like living stones, are being built into a spiritual house to be a holy priesthood, offering spiritual sacrifices acceptable to God through Jesus Christ.

1 Peter 2:5

Your Hourly Obedience to God

Now if you obey me fully and keep my covenant, then out of all nations you will be my treasured possession. Although the whole earth is mine.

Exodus 19:5

So if you faithfully obey the commands I am giving you today — to love the LORD your God and to serve him with all your heart and with all your soul — then I will send rain on your land in its season, both autumn and spring rains, so that you may gather in your grain, new wine and oil.

Deuteronomy 11:13,14

If you listen carefully to what he says and do all that I say, I will be an enemy to your enemies and will oppose those who oppose you. My angel will go ahead of you.

Exodus 23:22,23a

Blessed is the man who does not walk in the counsel of the wicked or stand in the way of sinners or sit in the seat of mockers.

But his delight is in the law of the LORD, and on his law he meditates day and night.

Psalm 1:1,2

All the ways of the LORD are loving and faithful for those who keep the demands of his covenant.

Psalm 25:10

The fear of the LORD is the beginning of wisdom; all who follow his precepts have good understanding. To him belongs eternal praise.

Psalm 111:10

Blessed are they who keep his statutes and seek him with all their heart. You have laid down precepts that are to be fully obeyed.

Psalm 119:2,4

Keep my commands and you will live; guard my teachings as the apple of your eye.

Proverbs 7:2

He who obeys instructions guards his life, but he who is contemptuous of his ways will die.

Proverbs 19:16

If you are willing and obedient, you will eat the best from the land.

Isaiah 1:19

Anyone who breaks one of the least of these commandments and teaches others to do the same will be called least in the kingdom of heaven, but whoever practices and teaches these commands will be called great in the kingdom of heaven.

Matthew 5:19

For whoever does the will of my Father in heaven is my brother and sister and mother.

Matthew 12:50

His master replied, "Well done, good and faithful servant! You have been faithful with a few things; I will put you in charge of many things. Come and share your master's happiness!"

Matthew 25:21

Whoever can be trusted with very little can also be trusted with much, and whoever is dishonest with very little will also be dishonest with much.
So if you have not been trustworthy in handling worldly wealth, who will trust you with true riches?

And if you have not been trustworthy with someone else's property, who will give you property of your own?

Luke 16:10-12

"If you love me, you will obey what I command."

Jesus replied, "If anyone loves me, he will obey my teaching. My Father will love him, and we will come to him and make our home with him."

John 14:15,23

If you obey my commands, you will remain in my love, just as I have obeyed my Father's commands and remain in his love. You are my friends if you do what I command.

John 15:10,14

Peter and the other apostles replied: "We must obey God rather than men!"

Acts 5:29

Although he was a son, he learned obedience from what he suffered and, once made perfect, he became the source of eternal salvation for all who obey him.

Hebrews 5:8,9

Submit yourselves, then, to God. Resist the devil, and he will flee from you.

James 4:7

And receive from him anything we ask, because we obey his commands and do what pleases him.

Those who obey his commands live in him, and he in them. And this is how we know that he lives in us: We know it by the Spirit he gave us.

1 John 3:22,24

Your Attitude

The Businesswoman and Faith

Those who know your name will trust in you, for you, LORD, have never forsaken those who seek you.

Psalm 9:10

Trust in the LORD and do good; dwell in the land and enjoy safe pasture.

Delight yourself in the LORD and he will give you the desires of your heart.

Commit your way to the LORD; trust in him and he will do this:

He will make your righteousness shine like the dawn, the justice of your cause like the noonday sun.

Psalm 37:3-6

You will keep in perfect peace him whose mind is steadfast, because he trusts in you.

Isaiah 26:3

But blessed is the man who trusts in the LORD, whose confidence is in him.

Jeremiah 17:7

When he had gone indoors, the blind men came to him, and he asked them, "Do you believe that I am able to do this?" "Yes, Lord," they replied.

Then he touched their eyes and said, "According to your faith will it be done to you."

Matthew 9:28,29

He replied, "Because you have so little faith. I tell you the truth, if you have faith as small as a mustard seed, you can say to this mountain, 'Move from here to there' and it will move. Nothing will be impossible for you."

Matthew 17:20

If you believe, you will receive whatever you ask for in prayer.

Matthew 21:22

"If you can?" said Jesus. "Everything is possible for him who believes."

Mark 9:23

"Have faith in God," Jesus answered.

"I tell you the truth, if anyone says to this mountain, 'Go, throw yourself into the sea,' and does not doubt in his heart but believes that what he says will happen, it will be done for him.

Therefore I tell you, whatever you ask for in prayer, believe that you have received it, and it will be yours."

Mark 11:22-24

Consequently, faith comes from hearing the message, and the message is heard through the word of Christ.

Romans 10:17

For by the grace given me I say to every one of you: Do not think of yourself more highly than you ought, but rather think of yourself with sober judgment, in accordance with the measure of faith God has given you.

Romans 12:3

In addition to all this, take up the shield of faith, with which you can extinguish all the flaming arrows of the evil one.

Ephesians 6:16

So do not throw away your confidence; it will be richly rewarded.

Hebrews 10:35

Now faith is being sure of what we hope for and certain of what we do not see.

And without faith it is impossible to please God, because anyone who comes to him must believe that he exists and that he rewards those who earnestly seek him.

Hebrews 11:1,6

Let us fix our eyes on Jesus, the author and perfecter of our faith, who for the joy set before him endured the cross, scorning its shame, and sat down at the right hand of the throne of God.

Hebrews 12:2

Keep your lives free from the love of money and be content with what you have, because God has said, "Never will I leave you; never will I forsake you."

So we say with confidence, "The Lord is my helper; I will not be afraid. What can man do to me?"

Hebrews 13:5,6

Look! The wages you failed to pay the workmen who mowed your fields are crying out against you. The cries of the harvesters have reached the ears of the Lord Almighty.

And the prayer offered in faith will make the sick person well; the Lord will raise him up. If he has sinned, he will be forgiven.

James 5:4,15

These have come so that your faith — of greater worth than gold, which perishes even though refined by fire — may be proved genuine and may result in praise, glory and honor when Jesus Christ is revealed.

Though you have not seen him, you love him; and even though you do not see him now, you believe in him and are filled with an inexpressible and glorious joy, for you are receiving the goal of your faith, the salvation of your souls.

1 Peter 1:7-9

For everyone born of God overcomes the world. This is the victory that has overcome the world, even our faith.

1 John 5:4

The Businesswoman and Wisdom

Therefore wisdom and knowledge will be given you. And I will also give you wealth, riches and honor, such as no king who was before you ever had and none after you will have.

2 Chronicles 1:12

So give your servant a discerning heart to govern your people and to distinguish between right and wrong. For who is able to govern this great people of yours?

1 Kings 3:9

Blessed is the man who does not walk in the counsel of the wicked or stand in the way of sinners or sit in the seat of mockers.

But his delight is in the law of the LORD, and on his law he meditates day and night.

He is like a tree planted by streams of water, which yields its fruit in season and whose leaf does not wither. Whatever he does prospers.

Psalm 1:1-3

I will praise the LORD, who counsels me; even at night my heart instructs me.

Psalm 16:7

Teach me your way, O LORD; lead me in a straight path because of my oppressors.

Psalm 27:11

Show me, O LORD, my life's end and the number of my days; let me know how fleeting is my life.

Psalm 39:4

Send forth your light and your truth, let them guide me; let them bring me to your holy mountain, to the place where you dwell.

Psalm 43:3

For the LORD gives wisdom, and from his mouth come knowledge and understanding.

Proverbs 2:6

Trust in the LORD with all your heart and lean not on your own understanding; in all your ways acknowledge him, and he will make your paths straight.

Proverbs 3:5,6

Wisdom is supreme; therefore get wisdom. Though it cost all you have, get understanding.
Esteem her, and she will exalt you; embrace her, and she will honor you.

Proverbs 4:7,8

Whoever loves discipline loves knowledge, but he who hates correction is stupid.

Proverbs 12:1

He who walks with the wise grows wise, but a companion of fools suffers harm.

Proverbs 13:20

Whoever gives heed to instruction prospers, and blessed is he who trusts in the LORD.

The wise in heart are called discerning, and pleasant words promote instruction.

Understanding is a fountain of life to those who have it, but folly brings punishment to fools.

A wise man's heart guides his mouth, and his lips promote instruction.

Proverbs 16:20-23

By wisdom a house is built, and through understanding it is established; through knowledge its rooms are filled with rare and beautiful treasures.

Proverbs 24:3,4

Be wise, my son, and bring joy to my heart; then I can answer anyone who treats me with contempt.

Proverbs 27:11

To the man who pleases him, God gives wisdom, knowledge and happiness, but to the sinner he gives the task of gathering and storing up wealth to hand it over to the one who pleases God. This too is meaningless, a chasing after the wind.

Ecclesiastes 2:26

Whether you turn to the right or to the left, your ears will hear a voice behind you, saying, "This is the way; walk in it."

Isaiah 30:21

He will be the sure foundation for your times, a rich store of salvation and wisdom and knowledge; the fear of the LORD is the key to this treasure.

Isaiah 33:6

If you believe, you will receive whatever you ask for in prayer.

Matthew 21:22

Who is wise? He will realize these things. Who is discerning? He will understand them. The ways of the LORD are right; the righteous walk in them, but the rebellious stumble in them.

Hosea 14:9

For I will give you words and wisdom that none of your adversaries will be able to resist or contradict.

Luke 21:15

But when he, the Spirit of truth, comes, he will guide you into all truth. He will not speak on his own; he will speak only what he hears, and he will tell you what is yet to come.

He will bring glory to me by taking from what is mine and making it known to you.

John 16:13,14

To one there is given through the Spirit the message of wisdom, to another the message of knowledge by means of the same Spirit.

1 Corinthians 12:8

I have not stopped giving thanks for you, remembering you in my prayers.

I keep asking that the God of our Lord Jesus Christ, the glorious Father, may give you the Spirit of wisdom and revelation, so that you may know him better.

I pray also that the eyes of your heart may be enlightened in order that you may know the hope to which he has called you, the riches of his glorious inheritance in the saints.

Ephesians 1:16-18

For this reason, since the day we heard about you, we have not stopped praying for you and asking God to fill you with the knowledge of his will through all spiritual wisdom and understanding.

And we pray this in order that you may live a life worthy of the Lord and may please him in every way: bearing fruit in every good work, growing in the knowledge of God.

Colossians 1:9,10

For God did not give us a spirit of timidity, but a spirit of power, of love and of self-discipline.

2 Timothy 1:7

If any of you lacks wisdom, he should ask God, who gives generously to all without finding fault, and it will be given to him.

James 1:5

The Businesswoman and Strength

For the joy of the LORD is your strength.

Nehemiah 8:10b

May the LORD answer you when you are in distress; may the name of the God of Jacob protect you.

May he send you help from the sanctuary and grant you support from Zion.

Psalm 20:1,2

The LORD is my rock, my fortress and my deliverer; my God is my rock, in whom I take refuge. He is my shield and the horn of my salvation, my stronghold.

Psalm 18:2

The LORD is my light and my salvation — whom shall I fear? The LORD is the stronghold of my life — of whom shall I be afraid?

Wait for the LORD; be strong and take heart and wait for the LORD.

Psalm 27:1,14

Be strong and take heart, all you who hope in the LORD.

Psalm 31:24

Be my rock of refuge, to which I can always go; give the command to save me, for you are my rock and my fortress.

Psalm 71:3

My soul is weary with sorrow; strengthen me according to your word.

Psalm 119:28

When I called, you answered me; you made me bold and stouthearted.

Psalm 138:3

Counsel and sound judgment are mine; I have understanding and power.

Proverbs 8:14

The way of the LORD is a refuge for the righteous, but it is the ruin of those who do evil.

Proverbs 10:29

He who fears the LORD has a secure fortress, and for his children it will be a refuge.

Proverbs 14:26

A wise man has great power, and a man of knowledge increases strength.

Proverbs 24:5

Surely God is my salvation; I will trust and not be afraid. The LORD, the LORD, is my strength and my song; he has become my salvation.

Isaiah 12:2

This is what the Sovereign LORD, the Holy One of Israel, says: "In repentance and rest is your salvation, in quietness and trust is your strength, but you would have none of it."

Isaiah 30:15

He gives strength to the weary and increases the power of the weak.
But those who hope in the LORD will renew their strength. They will soar on wings like eagles; they will run and not grow weary, they will walk and not be faint.

Isaiah 40:29,31

So do not fear, for I am with you; do not be dismayed, for I am your God. I will strengthen you and help you; I will uphold you with my righteous right hand.

Isaiah 41:10

"Do not be afraid, O man highly esteemed," he said. "Peace! Be strong now; be strong." When he spoke to me, I was strengthened and said, "Speak, my lord, since you have given me strength."

Daniel 10:19

The Sovereign LORD is my strength; he makes my feet like the feet of a deer, he enables me to go on the heights. For the director of music. On my stringed instruments.

Habakkuk 3:19

That is why, for Christ's sake, I delight in weaknesses, in insults, in hardships, in persecutions, in difficulties. For when I am weak, then I am strong.

2 Corinthians 12:10

I pray that out of his glorious riches he may strengthen you with power through his Spirit in your inner being, so that Christ may dwell in your hearts through faith.

Ephesians 3:16,17a

I can do everything through him who gives me strength.

Philippians 4:13

And we pray this in order that you may live a life worthy of the Lord and may please him in every way: bearing fruit in every good work, growing in the knowledge of God, being strengthened with all power according to his glorious might so that you may have great endurance and patience, and joyfully giving thanks to the Father, who has qualified you to share in the inheritance of the saints in the kingdom of light.

Colossians 1:10-12

The Businesswoman and Peace of Mind

I will lie down and sleep in peace, for you alone, O LORD, make me dwell in safety.

Psalm 4:8

The LORD gives strength to his people; the LORD blesses his people with peace.

Psalm 29:11

But the meek will inherit the land and enjoy great peace.
Consider the blameless, observe the upright; there is a future for the man of peace.

Psalm 37:11,37

I will listen to what God the LORD will say; he promises peace to his people, his saints — but let them not return to folly.

Psalm 85:8

Great peace have they who love your law, and nothing can make them stumble.

Psalm 119:165

Better one handful with tranquillity than two handfuls with toil and chasing after the wind.

Ecclesiastes 4:6

You will keep in perfect peace him whose mind is steadfast, because he trusts in you.

LORD, you establish peace for us; all that we have accomplished you have done for us.

Isaiah 26:3,12

You will go out in joy and be led forth in peace; the mountains and hills will burst into song before you, and all the trees of the field will clap their hands.

Isaiah 55:12

Those who walk uprightly enter into peace; they find rest as they lie in death.

Isaiah 57:2

Peace I leave with you; my peace I give you. I do not give to you as the world gives. Do not let your hearts be troubled and do not be afraid.

John 14:27

I have told you these things, so that in me you may have peace. In this world you will have trouble. But take heart! I have overcome the world.

John 16:33

Therefore, since we have been justified through faith, we have peace with God through our Lord Jesus Christ.

Romans 5:1

The mind of sinful man is death, but the mind controlled by the Spirit is life and peace.

Romans 8:6

May the God of hope fill you with all joy and peace as you trust in him, so that you may overflow with hope by the power of the Holy Spirit.

Romans 15:13

Finally, brothers, good-by. Aim for perfection, listen to my appeal, be of one mind, live in peace. And the God of love and peace will be with you.

2 Corinthians 13:11

Grace and peace to you from God our Father and the Lord Jesus Christ.

Galatians 1:3

But the fruit of the Spirit is love, joy, peace, patience, kindness, goodness, faithfulness.

Galatians 5:22

For he himself is our peace, who has made the two one and has destroyed the barrier, the dividing wall of hostility.

Ephesians 2:14

Do not be anxious about anything, but in everything, by prayer and petition, with thanksgiving, present your requests to God.

And the peace of God, which transcends all understanding, will guard your hearts and your minds in Christ Jesus.

Whatever you have learned or received or heard from me, or seen in me — put it into practice. And the God of peace will be with you.

Philippians 4:6,7,9

Let the peace of Christ rule in your hearts, since as members of one body you were called to peace. And be thankful.

Colossians 3:15

Now may the Lord of peace himself give you peace at all times and in every way. The Lord be with all of you.

2 Thessalonians 3:16

The Businesswoman and Integrity

As for you, if you walk before me in integrity of heart and uprightness, as David your father did, and do all I command and observe my decrees and laws, I will establish your royal throne over Israel forever, as I promised David your father when I said, "You shall never fail to have a man on the throne of Israel."

1 Kings 9:4,5

Let God weigh me in honest scales and he will know that I am blameless.

Job 31:6

Blessed is the man who does not walk in the counsel of the wicked or stand in the way of sinners or sit in the seat of mockers.

But his delight is in the law of the LORD, and on his law he meditates day and night.

Psalm 1:1,2

All the ways of the LORD are loving and faithful for those who keep the demands of his covenant.

May integrity and uprightness protect me, because my hope is in you.

Psalm 25:10,21

Vindicate me, O LORD, for I have led a blameless life; I have trusted in the LORD without wavering.

Psalm 26:1

In my integrity you uphold me and set me in your presence forever.

Psalm 41:12

And David shepherded them with integrity of heart; with skillful hands he led them.

Psalm 78:72

Good will come to him who is generous and lends freely, who conducts his affairs with justice.

Psalm 112:5

Blessed are they who keep his statutes and seek him with all their heart.

You have laid down precepts that are to be fully obeyed.

Psalm 119:2,4

The LORD abhors dishonest scales, but accurate weights are his delight.

The integrity of the upright guides them, but the unfaithful are destroyed by their duplicity.

Proverbs 11:1,3

Better a little with righteousness than much gain with injustice.

Proverbs 16:8

Better a poor man whose walk is blameless than a fool whose lips are perverse.

He who obeys instructions guards his life, but he who is contemptuous of his ways will die.

Proverbs 19:1,16

The righteous man leads a blameless life; blessed are his children after him.

Proverbs 20:7

A fortune made by a lying tongue is a fleeting vapor and a deadly snare.

Proverbs 21:6

If you are willing and obedient, you will eat the best from the land.

Isaiah 1:19

Do not repay anyone evil for evil. Be careful to do what is right in the eyes of everybody.

Romans 12:17

The Businesswoman and Commitment

Now fear the LORD and serve him with all faithfulness. Throw away the gods your forefathers worshiped beyond the River and in Egypt, and serve the LORD.

Joshua 24:14

Into your hands I commit my spirit; redeem me, O LORD, the God of truth.

Psalm 31:5

Commit your way to the LORD; trust in him and he will do this:
He will make your righteousness shine like the dawn, the justice of your cause like the noonday sun.

Psalm 37:5,6

Teach me your way, O LORD, and I will walk in your truth; give me an undivided heart, that I may fear your name.

Psalm 86:11

Blessed are they who keep his statutes and seek him with all their heart.
Give me understanding, and I will keep your law and obey it with all my heart.

Psalm 119:2,34

Blessed are all who fear the LORD, who walk in his ways.
You will eat the fruit of your labor; blessings and prosperity will be yours.

Psalm 128:1,2

Teach me to do your will, for you are my God; may your good Spirit lead me on level ground.

Psalm 143:10

Trust in the LORD with all your heart and lean not on your own understanding.

Proverbs 3:5

When you make a vow to God, do not delay in fulfilling it. He has no pleasure in fools; fulfill your vow.

It is better not to vow than to make a vow and not fulfill it.

Ecclesiastes 5:4,5

You will seek me and find me when you seek me with all your heart.

Jeremiah 29:13

Jesus replied: ''Love the Lord your God with all your heart and with all your soul and with all your mind.''

Matthew 22:37

But the one who does not know and does things deserving punishment will be beaten with few blows. From everyone who has been given much, much will be demanded; and from the one who has been entrusted with much, much more will be asked.

Luke 12:48

If anyone comes to me and does not hate his father and mother, his wife and children, his brothers and sisters — yes, even his own life — he cannot be my disciple.

And anyone who does not carry his cross and follow me cannot be my disciple.

In the same way, any of you who does not give up everything he has cannot be my disciple.
Luke 14:26,27,33

"I tell you the truth," Jesus said to them, "no one who has left home or wife or brothers or parents or children for the sake of the kingdom of God will fail to receive many times as much in this age and, in the age to come, eternal life."
Luke 18:29,30

Do not offer the parts of your body to sin, as instruments of wickedness, but rather offer yourselves to God, as those who have been brought from death to life; and offer the parts of your body to him as instruments of righteousness.
Romans 6:13

For if you live according to the sinful nature, you will die; but if by the Spirit you put to death the misdeeds of the body, you will live.
Romans 8:13

Therefore, I urge you, brothers, in view of God's mercy, to offer your bodies as living sacrifices, holy and pleasing to God — this is your spiritual act of worship.
Do not conform any longer to the pattern of this world, but be transformed by the renewing of your mind. Then you will be able to test and approve what God's will is — his good, pleasing and perfect will.

Romans 12:1,2

I have been crucified with Christ and I no longer live, but Christ lives in me. The life I live in the body, I live by faith in the Son of God, who loved me and gave himself for me.

Galatians 2:20

But whatever was to my profit I now consider loss for the sake of Christ.

What is more, I consider everything a loss compared to the surpassing greatness of knowing Christ Jesus my Lord, for whose sake I have lost all things. I consider them rubbish, that I may gain Christ.

Philippians 3:7,8

If a man cleanses himself from the latter, he will be an instrument for noble purposes, made holy, useful to the Master and prepared to do any good work.

2 Timothy 2:21

The Businesswoman and Ambition

Lazy hands make a man poor, but diligent hands bring wealth.

Proverbs 10:4

The sluggard craves and gets nothing, but the desires of the diligent are fully satisfied.

Proverbs 13:4

The plans of the diligent lead to profit as surely as haste leads to poverty.

Proverbs 21:5

Do you see a man skilled in his work? He will serve before kings; he will not serve before obscure men.

Proverbs 22:29

Be sure you know the condition of your flocks, give careful attention to your herds.

Proverbs 27:23

Whatever your hand finds to do, do it with all your might, for in the grave, where you are going, there is neither working nor planning nor knowledge nor wisdom.

Ecclesiastes 9:10

In the same way, let your light shine before men, that they may see your good deeds and praise your Father in heaven.

Matthew 5:16

But seek first his kingdom and his righteousness, and all these things will be given to you as well.

Matthew 6:33

Make every effort to enter through the narrow door, because many, I tell you, will try to enter and will not be able to.

Luke 13:24

Do you not know that in a race all the runners run, but only one gets the prize? Run in such a way as to get the prize.

Everyone who competes in the games goes into strict training. They do it to get a crown that will not last; but we do it to get a crown that will last forever.

1 Corinthians 9:24,25

Brothers, I do not consider myself yet to have taken hold of it. But one thing I do: Forgetting what is behind and straining toward what is ahead, I press on toward the goal to win the prize for which God has called me heavenward in Christ Jesus.

Philippians 3:13,14

Command those who are rich in this present world not to be arrogant nor to put their hope in wealth, which is so uncertain, but to put their hope in God, who richly provides us with everything for our enjoyment.

1 Timothy 6:17

Do your best to present yourself to God as one approved, a workman who does not need to be ashamed and who correctly handles the word of truth.

2 Timothy 2:15

Our people must learn to devote themselves to doing what is good, in order that they may provide for daily necessities and not live unproductive lives.

Titus 3:14

God is not unjust; he will not forget your work and the love you have shown him as you have helped his people and continue to help them.

Hebrews 6:10

The Businesswoman and Leadership

If the LORD delights in a man's way, he makes his steps firm.

Psalm 37:23

For the LORD God is a sun and shield; the LORD bestows favor and honor; no good thing does he withhold from those whose walk is blameless.

Psalm 84:11

Good will come to him who is generous and lends freely, who conducts his affairs with justice.

Psalm 112:5

Better a little with righteousness than much gain with injustice.

In his heart a man plans his course, but the LORD determines his steps.

Proverbs 16:8,9

Whether you turn to the right or to the left, your ears will hear a voice behind you, saying, "This is the way; walk in it."

Isaiah 30:21

This is what the LORD Almighty says: "Administer true justice; show mercy and compassion to one another.

Do not oppress the widow or the fatherless, the alien or the poor. In your hearts do not think evil of each other.''

Zechariah 7:9,10

For in the same way you judge others, you will be judged, and with the measure you use, it will be measured to you.

Matthew 7:2

But when he, the Spirit of truth, comes, he will guide you into all truth. He will not speak on his own; he will speak only what he hears, and he will tell you what is yet to come.

John 16:13

Because those who are led by the Spirit of God are sons of God.

Romans 8:14

For kings and all those in authority, that we may live peaceful and quiet lives in all godliness and holiness.

1 Timothy 2:2

The Businesswoman and Respect

If the LORD delights in a man's way, he makes his steps firm.

Psalm 37:23

For the LORD God is a sun and shield; the LORD bestows favor and honor; no good thing does he withhold from those whose walk is blameless.

Psalm 84:11

A good man obtains favor from the LORD, but the LORD condemns a crafty man.

Proverbs 12:2

A good man leaves an inheritance for his children's children, but a sinner's wealth is stored up for the righteous.

Proverbs 13:22

A good name is more desirable than great riches; to be esteemed is better than silver or gold.

Proverbs 22:1

The wicked man flees though no one pursues, but the righteous are as bold as a lion.

Proverbs 28:1

A good name is better than fine perfume, and the day of death better than the day of birth.

Ecclesiastes 7:1

In the same way, let your light shine before men, that they may see your good deeds and praise your Father in heaven.

Matthew 5:16

A student is not above his teacher, nor a servant above his master.

Matthew 10:24

The good man brings good things out of the good stored up in his heart, and the evil man brings evil things out of the evil stored up in his heart. For out of the overflow of his heart his mouth speaks.

Luke 6:45

For, "Whoever would love life and see good days must keep his tongue from evil and his lips from deceitful speech.. He must turn from evil and do good; he must seek peace and pursue it."

1 Peter 3:10,11

Do not allow what you consider good to be spoken of as evil.

Romans 14:16

The Businesswoman and a Servant's Heart

As the eyes of slaves look to the hand of their master, as the eyes of a maid look to the hand of her mistress, so our eyes look to the LORD our God, till he shows us his mercy.

Psalm 123:2

Like the coolness of snow at harvest time is a trustworthy messenger to those who send him; he refreshes the spirit of his masters.

Proverbs 25:13

He who tends a fig tree will eat its fruit, and he who looks after his master will be honored.

Proverbs 27:18

Whatever your hand finds to do, do it with all your might.

Ecclesiastes 9:10b

When the king heard this, he was greatly distressed; he was determined to rescue Daniel and made every effort until sundown to save him.

Daniel 6:14

In the same way, let your light shine before men, that they may see your good deeds and praise your Father in heaven.

Matthew 5:16

And if anyone gives even a cup of cold water to one of these little ones because he is my disciple, I tell you the truth, he will certainly not lose his reward.

Matthew 10:42

Just as the Son of Man did not come to be served, but to serve, and to give his life as a ransom for many.

Matthew 20:28

Who then is the faithful and wise servant, whom the master has put in charge of the servants in his household to give them their food at the proper time?

It will be good for that servant whose master finds him doing so when he returns.

I tell you the truth, he will put him in charge of all his possessions.

Matthew 24:45-47

Not so with you. Instead, whoever wants to become great among you must be your servant, and whoever wants to be first must be slave of all.

Mark 10:43,44

"Which of these three do you think was a neighbor to the man who fell into the hands of robbers?"

The expert in the law replied, "The one who had mercy on him." Jesus told him, "Go and do likewise."

Luke 10:36,37

The Lord answered, "Who then is the faithful and wise manager, whom the master puts in charge of his servants to give them their food allowance at the proper time?"

Luke 12:42

No servant can serve two masters. Either he will hate the one and love the other, or he will be devoted to the one and despise the other. You cannot serve both God and Money.

Luke 16:13

For who is greater, the one who is at the table or the one who serves? Is it not the one who is at the table? But I am among you as one who serves.
Luke 22:27

I tell you the truth, no servant is greater than his master, nor is a messenger greater than the one who sent him.
John 13:16

Carry each other's burdens, and in this way you will fulfill the law of Christ.

Therefore, as we have opportunity, let us do good to all people, especially to those who belong to the family of believers.
Galatians 6:2,10

Slaves, obey your earthly masters with respect and fear, and with sincerity of heart, just as you would obey Christ.

Obey them not only to win their favor when their eye is on you, but like slaves of Christ, doing the will of God from your heart.

Serve wholeheartedly, as if you were serving the Lord, not men.
Ephesians 6:5-7

Slaves, obey your earthly masters in everything; and do it, not only when their eye is on you and to win their favor, but with sincerity of heart and reverence for the Lord.

Whatever you do, work at it with all your heart, as working for the Lord, not for men.
Colossians 3:22,23

The Businesswoman and Honesty

Now if you obey me fully and keep my covenant, then out of all nations you will be my treasured possession. Although the whole earth is mine.

Exodus 19:5

Blessed is the man who does not walk in the counsel of the wicked or stand in the way of sinners or sit in the seat of mockers.

But his delight is in the law of the LORD, and on his law he meditates day and night.

Psalm 1:1,2

All the ways of the LORD are loving and faithful for those who keep the demands of his covenant.

Psalm 25:10

Blessed are they who keep his statutes and seek him with all their heart.

You have laid down precepts that are to be fully obeyed.

Psalm 119:2,4

Vindicate me, O LORD, for I have led a blameless life; I have trusted in the LORD without wavering.

Psalm 26:1

In my integrity you uphold me and set me in your presence forever.

Psalm 41:12

And David shepherded them with integrity of heart; with skillful hands he led them.

Psalm 78:72

The LORD abhors dishonest scales, but accurate weights are his delight.

The integrity of the upright guides them, but the unfaithful are destroyed by their duplicity.

Proverbs 11:1,3

Better a poor man whose walk is blameless than a fool whose lips are perverse.

He who obeys instructions guards his life, but he who is contemptuous of his ways will die.

Proverbs 19:1,16

The righteous man leads a blameless life; blessed are his children after him.

Proverbs 20:7

If you are willing and obedient, you will eat the best from the land.

Isaiah 1:19

Do to others as you would have them do to you.

Luke 6:31

Rather, we have renounced secret and shameful ways; we do not use deception, nor do we distort the word of God. On the contrary, by setting forth the truth plainly we commend ourselves to every man's conscience in the sight of God.

2 Corinthians 4:2

For we are taking pains to do what is right, not only in the eyes of the Lord but also in the eyes of men.

2 Corinthians 8:21

Do not repay anyone evil for evil. Be careful to do what is right in the eyes of everybody.

Romans 12:17

Finally, brothers, whatever is true, whatever is noble, whatever is right, whatever is pure, whatever is lovely, whatever is admirable — if anything is excellent or praiseworthy — think about such things.

Philippians 4:8

So that your daily life may win the respect of outsiders and so that you will not be dependent on anybody.

1 Thessalonians 4:12

Live such good lives among the pagans that, though they accuse you of doing wrong, they may see your good deeds and glorify God on the day he visits us.

1 Peter 2:12

The Businesswoman and an Achiever's Attitude

Have I not commanded you? Be strong and courageous. Do not be terrified; do not be discouraged, for the LORD your God will be with you wherever you go.

Joshua 1:9

But as for you, be strong and do not give up, for your work will be rewarded.

2 Chronicles 15:7

For you have been my hope, O Sovereign LORD, my confidence since my youth.

Psalm 71:5

Good will come to him who is generous and lends freely, who conducts his affairs with justice.

Surely he will never be shaken; a righteous man will be remembered forever.

He will have no fear of bad news; his heart is steadfast, trusting in the LORD.

Psalm 112:5-7

But blessed is the man who trusts in the LORD, whose confidence is in him.

He will be like a tree planted by the water that sends out its roots by the stream. It does not fear when heat comes; its leaves are always green. It has no worries in a year of drought and never fails to bear fruit.

Jeremiah 17:7,8

"If you can?" said Jesus. "Everything is possible for him who believes."

Mark 9:23

He replied, "If you have faith as small as a mustard seed, you can say to this mulberry tree, 'Be uprooted and planted in the sea,' and it will obey you."

Luke 17:6

Not only so, but we also rejoice in our sufferings, because we know that suffering produces perseverance; perseverance, character; and character, hope.

And hope does not disappoint us, because God has poured out his love into our hearts by the Holy Spirit, whom he has given us.

Romans 5:3-5

May the God of hope fill you with all joy and peace as you trust in him, so that you may overflow with hope by the power of the Holy Spirit.

Romans 15:13

I press on toward the goal to win the prize for which God has called me heavenward in Christ Jesus.

Philippians 3:14

I can do everything through him who gives me strength.

Philippians 4:13

So do not throw away your confidence; it will be richly rewarded.

Hebrews 10:35

The Businesswoman and Diligence

Lazy hands make a man poor, but diligent hands bring wealth.

He who gathers crops in summer is a wise son, but he who sleeps during harvest is a disgraceful son.

Proverbs 10:4,5

Diligent hands will rule, but laziness ends in slave labor.

The lazy man does not roast his game, but the diligent man prizes his possessions.
Proverbs 12:24,27

The sluggard craves and gets nothing, but the desires of the diligent are fully satisfied.
Proverbs 13:4

The plans of the diligent lead to profit as surely as haste leads to poverty.
Proverbs 21:5

Do you see a man skilled in his work? He will serve before kings; he will not serve before obscure men.
Proverbs 22:29

Be sure you know the condition of your flocks, give careful attention to your herds.
Proverbs 27:23

Whatever your hand finds to do, do it with all your might, for in the grave, where you are going, there is neither working nor planning nor knowledge nor wisdom.
Ecclesiastes 9:10

The Sovereign LORD has given me an instructed tongue, to know the word that sustains the weary. He wakens me morning by morning, wakens my ear to listen like one being taught.
Isaiah 50:4

But the one who does not know and does things deserving punishment will be beaten with few blows. From everyone who has been given much, much will be demanded; and from the one who has been entrusted with much, much more will be asked.

Luke 12:48

Do you not say, ''Four months more and then the harvest''? I tell you, open your eyes and look at the fields! They are ripe for harvest.

John 4:35

As long as it is day, we must do the work of him who sent me. Night is coming, when no one can work.

John 9:4

Therefore, my dear brothers, stand firm. Let nothing move you. Always give yourselves fully to the work of the Lord, because you know that your labor in the Lord is not in vain.

1 Corinthians 15:58

I can do everything through him who gives me strength.

Philippians 4:13

Be wise in the way you act toward outsiders; make the most of every opportunity.

Colossians 4:5

We want each of you to show this same diligence to the very end, in order to make your hope sure.

We do not want you to become lazy, but to imitate those who through faith and patience inherit what has been promised.

Hebrews 6:11,12

So then, dear friends, since you are looking forward to this, make every effort to be found spotless, blameless and at peace with him.

2 Peter 3:14

I know your deeds. See, I have placed before you an open door that no one can shut. I know that you have little strength, yet you have kept my word and have not denied my name.

Revelation 3:8

The Businesswoman and Loyalty

And if you walk in my ways and obey my statutes and commands as David your father did, I will give you a long life.

1 Kings 3:14

Blessed is the man who does not walk in the counsel of the wicked or stand in the way of sinners or sit in the seat of mockers.But his delight is in the law of the LORD, and on his law he meditates day and night.

Psalm 1:1,2

All the ways of the LORD are loving and faithful for those who keep the demands of his covenant.

Psalm 25:10

The fear of the LORD is the beginning of wisdom; all who follow his precepts have good understanding. To him belongs eternal praise.

Psalm 111:10

Blessed are they who keep his statutes and seek him with all their heart. You have laid down precepts that are to be fully obeyed.

Psalm 119:2,4

Vindicate me, O LORD, for I have led a blameless life; I have trusted in the LORD without wavering.

Psalm 26:1

In my integrity you uphold me and set me in your presence forever.

Psalm 41:12

And David shepherded them with integrity of heart; with skillful hands he led them.

Psalm 78:72

The LORD abhors dishonest scales, but accurate weights are his delight.

When pride comes, then comes disgrace, but with humility comes wisdom.

The integrity of the upright guides them, but the unfaithful are destroyed by their duplicity.

Proverbs 11:1-3

Better a poor man whose walk is blameless than a fool whose lips are perverse.

He who obeys instructions guards his life, but he who is contemptuous of his ways will die.
Proverbs 19:1,16

The righteous man leads a blameless life; blessed are his children after him.
Proverbs 20:7

If you are willing and obedient, you will eat the best from the land.
Isaiah 1:19

Do to others as you would have them do to you.
Luke 6:31

Rather, we have renounced secret and shameful ways; we do not use deception, nor do we distort the word of God. On the contrary, by setting forth the truth plainly we commend ourselves to every man's conscience in the sight of God.
2 Corinthians 4:2

For we are taking pains to do what is right, not only in the eyes of the Lord but also in the eyes of men.
2 Corinthians 8:21

Do not repay anyone evil for evil. Be careful to do what is right in the eyes of everybody.
Romans 12:17

The Businesswoman and Decisiveness

Then Elijah said to him, "Stay here; the LORD has sent me to the Jordan." And he replied, "As surely as the LORD lives and as you live, I will not leave you." So the two of them walked on.
2 Kings 2:6

But the child's mother said, ''As surely as the LORD lives and as you live, I will not leave you.'' So he got up and followed her.

2 Kings 4:30

So we rebuilt the wall till all of it reached half its height, for the people worked with all their heart.

Nehemiah 4:6

Our hearts had not turned back; our feet had not strayed from your path.

Psalm 44:18

Go to the ant, you sluggard; consider its ways and be wise!

It has no commander, no overseer or ruler, yet it stores its provisions in summer and gathers its food at harvest.

Proverbs 6:6-8

If you falter in times of trouble, how small is your strength!

Proverbs 24:10

Ants are creatures of little strength, yet they store up their food in the summer.

Proverbs 30:25

Whatever your hand finds to do, do it with all your might, for in the grave, where you are going, there is neither working nor planning nor knowledge nor wisdom.

Ecclesiastes 9:10

Because the Sovereign LORD helps me, I will not be disgraced. Therefore have I set my face like flint, and I know I will not be put to shame.

Isaiah 50:7

They will be my people, and I will be their God.

I will give them singleness of heart and action, so that they will always fear me for their own good and the good of their children after them.

Jeremiah 32:38,39

Do not gloat over me, my enemy! Though I have fallen, I will rise. Though I sit in darkness, the LORD will be my light.

Micah 7:8

Ask and it will be given to you; seek and you will find; knock and the door will be opened to you.

For everyone who asks receives; he who seeks finds; and to him who knocks, the door will be opened.

Which of you, if his son asks for bread, will give him a stone?

Or if he asks for a fish, will give him a snake?

If you, then, though you are evil, know how to give good gifts to your children, how much more will your Father in heaven give good gifts to those who ask him!

Matthew 7:7-11

Then Paul answered, "Why are you weeping and breaking my heart? I am ready not only to be bound, but also to die in Jerusalem for the name of the Lord Jesus."

Acts 21:13

The Businesswoman and Negotiation

Be strong and courageous. Do not be afraid or terrified because of them, for the LORD your God goes with you; he will never leave you nor forsake you.

Deuteronomy 31:6

Have I not commanded you? Be strong and courageous. Do not be terrified; do not be discouraged, for the LORD your God will be with you wherever you go.

Joshua 1:9

Wait for the LORD; be strong and take heart and wait for the LORD.

Psalm 27:14

A patient man has great understanding, but a quick-tempered man displays folly.

Proverbs 14:29

The tongue that brings healing is a tree of life, but a deceitful tongue crushes the spirit.

Proverbs 15:4

Starting a quarrel is like breaching a dam; so drop the matter before a dispute breaks out.

A man of knowledge uses words with restraint, and a man of understanding is even-tempered.

Proverbs 17:14,27

The end of a matter is better than its beginning, and patience is better than pride.

Ecclesiastes 7:8

The Spirit of the LORD will rest on him — the Spirit of wisdom and of understanding, the Spirit of counsel and of power, the Spirit of knowledge and of the fear of the LORD.

Isaiah 11:2

But they could not stand up against his wisdom or the Spirit by whom he spoke.

Acts 6:10

Love must be sincere. Hate what is evil; cling to what is good.

Be devoted to one another in brotherly love. Honor one another above yourselves.

Never be lacking in zeal, but keep your spiritual fervor, serving the Lord.

If it is possible, as far as it depends on you, live at peace with everyone.

Romans 12:9-11,18

For God did not give us a spirit of timidity, but a spirit of power, of love and of self-discipline.

2 Timothy 1:7

If any of you lacks wisdom, he should ask God, who gives generously to all without finding fault, and it will be given to him.

James 1:5

But the wisdom that comes from heaven is first of all pure; then peace-loving, considerate, submissive, full of mercy and good fruit, impartial and sincere.

James 3:17

The Businesswoman and Goal-Setting

I, wisdom, dwell together with prudence; I possess knowledge and discretion.

Proverbs 8:12

He who brings trouble on his family will inherit only wind, and the fool will be servant to the wise.

Proverbs 11:29

A man is praised according to his wisdom, but men with warped minds are despised.

Proverbs 12:8

Every prudent man acts out of knowledge, but a fool exposes his folly.

Proverbs 13:16

A simple man believes anything, but a prudent man gives thought to his steps.
A wise man fears the LORD and shuns evil, but a fool is hotheaded and reckless.

Proverbs 14:15,16

Plans fail for lack of counsel, but with many advisers they succeed.

Proverbs 15:22

Whoever gives heed to instruction prospers, and blessed is he who trusts in the LORD.

Proverbs 16:20

The heart of the discerning acquires knowledge; the ears of the wise seek it out.

Proverbs 18:15

The purposes of a man's heart are deep waters, but a man of understanding draws them out. Make plans by seeking advice; if you wage war, obtain guidance.

Proverbs 20:5,18

The plans of the diligent lead to profit as surely as haste leads to poverty.

Proverbs 21:5

For waging war you need guidance, and for victory many advisers.

Proverbs 24:6

The prudent see danger and take refuge, but the simple keep going and suffer for it.

Proverbs 27:12

If the ax is dull and its edge unsharpened, more strength is needed but skill will bring success.

Ecclesiastes 10:10

Who despises the day of small things? Men will rejoice when they see the plumb line in the hand of Zerubbabel. (These seven are the eyes of the LORD, which range throughout the earth.)

Zechariah 4:10

Ask and it will be given to you; seek and you will find; knock and the door will be opened to you.

Matthew 7:7

Suppose one of you wants to build a tower. Will he not first sit down and estimate the cost to see if he has enough money to complete it?

For if he lays the foundation and is not able to finish it, everyone who sees it will ridicule him, saying, "This fellow began to build and was not able to finish."

Or suppose a king is about to go to war against another king. Will he not first sit down and consider whether he is able with ten thousand men to oppose the one coming against him with twenty thousand?
Luke 14:28-31

But eagerly desire the greater gifts. And now I will show you the most excellent way.
1 Corinthians 12:31

Now to him who is able to do immeasurably more than all we ask or imagine, according to his power that is at work within us.
Ephesians 3:20

The Businesswoman and Motivation

No man will be able to stand against you. The LORD your God, as he promised you, will put the terror and fear of you on the whole land, wherever you go.
Deuteronomy 11:25

The LORD will grant that the enemies who rise up against you will be defeated before you. They will come at you from one direction but flee from you in seven.
Deuteronomy 28:7

Be strong and courageous. Do not be afraid or terrified because of them, for the LORD your God goes with you; he will never leave you nor forsake you.
Deuteronomy 31:6

Be strong and courageous, because you will lead these people to inherit the land I swore to their forefathers to give them.

Joshua 1:6

The LORD has driven out before you great and powerful nations; to this day no one has been able to withstand you.

Joshua 23:9

David was greatly distressed because the men were talking of stoning him; each one was bitter in spirit because of his sons and daughters. But David found strength in the LORD his God.

1 Samuel 30:6

"Don't be afraid," the prophet answered. "Those who are with us are more than those who are with them."

2 Kings 6:16

Through you we push back our enemies; through your name we trample our foes.

Psalm 44:5

Instruct a wise man and he will be wiser still; teach a righteous man and he will add to his learning.

Proverbs 9:9

If a man is lazy, the rafters sag; if his hands are idle, the house leaks.

Ecclesiastes 10:18

For I am the LORD, your God, who takes hold
of your right hand and says to you, Do not fear;
I will help you.

Isaiah 41:13

The Spirit of the Sovereign LORD is on me,
because the LORD has anointed me to preach good
news to the poor. He has sent me to bind up the
brokenhearted, to proclaim freedom for the
captives and release from darkness for the
prisoners.

Isaiah 61:1

Those who are wise will shine like the
brightness of the heavens, and those who lead many
to righteousness, like the stars for ever and ever.

Daniel 12:3

Ask and it will be given to you; seek and you
will find; knock and the door will be opened to you.

For everyone who asks receives; he who seeks
finds; and to him who knocks, the door will be
opened.

Matthew 7:7,8

And I tell you that you are Peter, and on this
rock I will build my church, and the gates of Hades
will not overcome it.

I will give you the keys of the kingdom of
heaven; whatever you bind on earth will be bound
in heaven, and whatever you loose on earth will
be loosed in heaven.

Matthew 16:18,19

Then you will know the truth, and the truth will set you free.

So if the Son sets you free, you will be free indeed.

John 8:32,36

I tell you the truth, anyone who has faith in me will do what I have been doing. He will do even greater things than these, because I am going to the Father.

John 14:12

But you will receive power when the Holy Spirit comes on you; and you will be my witnesses in Jerusalem, and in all Judea and Samaria, and to the ends of the earth.

Acts 1:8

The weapons we fight with are not the weapons of the world. On the contrary, they have divine power to demolish strongholds.

2 Corinthians 10:4

For it is light that makes everything visible. This is why it is said: "Wake up, O sleeper, rise from the dead, and Christ will shine on you."

Ephesians 5:14

I can do everything through him who gives me strength.

Philippians 4:13

Being strengthened with all power according to his glorious might so that you may have great endurance and patience, and joyfully giving thanks

to the Father, who has qualified you to share in the inheritance of the saints in the kingdom of light.
Colossians 1:11,12

Be wise in the way you act toward outsiders; make the most of every opportunity.
Colossians 4:5

Be diligent in these matters; give yourself wholly to them, so that everyone may see your progress.
1 Timothy 4:15

Therefore let us leave the elementary teachings about Christ and go on to maturity.
Hebrews 6:1a

You, dear children, are from God and have overcome them, because the one who is in you is greater than the one who is in the world.

We are from God, and whoever knows God listens to us; but whoever is not from God does not listen to us. This is how we recognize the Spirit of truth and the spirit of falsehood.

And so we know and rely on the love God has for us. God is love. Whoever lives in love lives in God, and God in him.

Love is made complete among us so that we will have confidence on the day of judgment, because in this world we are like him.
1 John 4:4,6,16,17

Dear friend, I pray that you may enjoy good health and that all may go well with you, even as your soul is getting along well.
3 John 1:2

The Businesswoman and New Ideas

Now go; I will help you speak and will teach you what to say.

Exodus 4:12

Be strong and very courageous. Be careful to obey all the law my servant Moses gave you; do not turn from it to the right or to the left, that you may be successful wherever you go.

Joshua 1:7

But it is the spirit in a man, the breath of the Almighty, that gives him understanding.

Job 32:8

He may speak in their ears and terrify them with warnings.

Job 33:16

I will praise the LORD, who counsels me; even at night my heart instructs me.

Psalm 16:7

I will instruct you and teach you in the way you should go; I will counsel you and watch over you.

Psalm 32:8

For with you is the fountain of life; in your light we see light.

Psalm 36:9

The LORD will fulfill for me; your love, O LORD, endures forever — do not abandon the works of your hands.

Psalm 138:8

Let the wise listen and add to their learning, and let the discerning get guidance.

Proverbs 1:5

Wisdom is supreme; therefore get wisdom. Though it cost all you have, get understanding.
Esteem her, and she will exalt you; embrace her, and she will honor you.

Proverbs 4:7,8

I love those who love me, and those who seek me find me.

Proverbs 8:17

With me are riches and honor, enduring wealth and prosperity.

Proverbs 8:18

Bestowing wealth on those who love me and making their treasuries full.

Proverbs 8:21

The plans of the righteous are just, but the advice of the wicked is deceitful.

Proverbs 12:5

He who walks with the wise grows wise, but a companion of fools suffers harm.

Proverbs 13:20

Know also that wisdom is sweet to your soul; if you find it, there is a future hope for you, and your hope will not be cut off.

Proverbs 24:14

See, the former things have taken place, and new things I declare; before they spring into being I announce them to you.

Isaiah 42:9

Forget the former things; do not dwell on the past.

See, I am doing a new thing! Now it springs up; do you not perceive it? I am making a way in the desert and streams in the wasteland.

Isaiah 43:18,19

You have heard these things; look at them all. Will you not admit them? From now on I will tell you of new things, of hidden things unknown to you.

They are created now, and not long ago; you have not heard of them before today. So you cannot say, "Yes, I knew of them."

Isaiah 48:6,7

The Sovereign LORD has given me an instructed tongue, to know the word that sustains the weary. He wakens me morning by morning, wakens my ear to listen like one being taught.

Isaiah 50:4

"For I know the plans I have for you," declares the LORD, "plans to prosper you and not to harm you, plans to give you hope and a future."

Jeremiah 29:11

Then the LORD replied: "Write down the revelation and make it plain on tablets so that a herald may run with it.

For the revelation awaits an appointed time; it speaks of the end and will not prove false. Though it linger, wait for it; it will certainly come and will not delay."

Habakkuk 2:2,3

Who despises the day of small things? Men will rejoice when they see the plumb line in the hand of Zerubbabel. (These seven are the eyes of the LORD, which range throughout the earth.)

Zechariah 4:10

Ask and it will be given to you; seek and you will find; knock and the door will be opened to you.

Matthew 7:7

Suppose one of you wants to build a tower. Will he not first sit down and estimate the cost to see if he has enough money to complete it?

Luke 14:28

Because you know that the Lord will reward everyone for whatever good he does, whether he is slave or free.

Ephesians 6:8

The Businesswoman and Wise Counsel

Blessed is the man who does not walk in the counsel of the wicked or stand in the way of sinners or sit in the seat of mockers.

But his delight is in the law of the LORD, and on his law he meditates day and night.

He is like a tree planted by streams of water, which yields its fruit in season and whose leaf does not wither. Whatever he does prospers.

Psalm 1:1-3

I will praise the LORD, who counsels me; even at night my heart instructs me.

Psalm 16:7

Show me your ways, O LORD, teach me your paths.

Psalm 25:4

Though an army besiege me, my heart will not fear; though war break out against me, even then will I be confident.

One thing I ask of the LORD, this is what I seek: that I may dwell in the house of the LORD all the days of my life, to gaze upon the beauty of the LORD and to seek him in his temple.

For in the day of trouble he will keep me safe in his dwelling; he will hide me in the shelter of his tabernacle and set me high upon a rock.

Psalm 27:3-5

I will instruct you and teach you in the way you should go; I will counsel you and watch over you.

Psalm 32:8

God is our refuge and strength, an ever-present help in trouble.

Psalm 46:1

Surely you desire truth in the inner parts; you teach me wisdom in the inmost place.

Psalm 51:6

I will say of the LORD, ''He is my refuge and my fortress, my God, in whom I trust.''

Psalm 91:2

Even in darkness light dawns for the upright, for the gracious and compassionate and righteous man.

Psalm 112:4

The LORD is with me; I will not be afraid. What can man do to me?

It is better to take refuge in the LORD than to trust in man.

Psalm 118:6,8

Your word, O LORD, is eternal; it stands firm in the heavens.

Psalm 119:89

For the LORD gives wisdom, and from his mouth come knowledge and understanding.

Proverbs 2:6

Trust in the LORD with all your heart and lean not on your own understanding; in all your ways acknowledge him, and he will make your paths straight.

Proverbs 3:5,6

My son, pay attention to what I say; listen closely to my words.
Do not let them out of your sight, keep them within your heart; for they are life to those who find them and health to a man's whole body.

Proverbs 4:20-22

For lack of guidance a nation falls, but many advisers make victory sure.

Proverbs 11:14

Plans fail for lack of counsel, but with many advisers they succeed.

Proverbs 15:22

Perfume and incense bring joy to the heart, and the pleasantness of one's friend springs from his earnest counsel.

Proverbs 27:9

Whether you turn to the right or to the left, your ears will hear a voice behind you, saying, ''This is the way; walk in it.''

Isaiah 30:21

The grass withers and the flowers fall, but the word of our God stands forever.

Isaiah 40:8

I will lead the blind by ways they have not known, along unfamiliar paths I will guide them; I will turn the darkness into light before them and make the rough places smooth. These are the things I will do; I will not forsake them.

Isaiah 42:16

This is what the LORD says — your Redeemer, the Holy One of Israel: ''I am the LORD your God, who teaches you what is best for you, who directs you in the way you should go.''

Isaiah 48:17

I tell you the truth, this generation will certainly not pass away until all these things have happened.

Matthew 24:34

But when he, the Spirit of truth, comes, he will guide you into all truth. He will not speak on his own; he will speak only what he hears, and he will tell you what is yet to come.

He will bring glory to me by taking from what is mine and making it known to you.

John 16:13,14

What, then, shall we say in response to this? If God is for us, who can be against us?

Romans 8:31

If any of you lacks wisdom, he should ask God, who gives generously to all without finding fault, and it will be given to him.

James 1:5

Your Work

When a Customer Is Dissatisfied

Refrain from anger and turn from wrath; do not fret — it leads only to evil.

Psalm 37:8

A gentle answer turns away wrath, but a harsh word stirs up anger.

A hot-tempered man stirs up dissension, but a patient man calms a quarrel.

Proverbs 15:1,18

The end of a matter is better than its beginning, and patience is better than pride.

Ecclesiastes 7:8

By standing firm you will gain life.

Luke 21:19

Be joyful in hope, patient in affliction, faithful in prayer.

Romans 12:12

Love is patient, love is kind. It does not envy, it does not boast, it is not proud.

It is not rude, it is not self-seeking, it is not easily angered, it keeps no record of wrongs.

1 Corinthians 13:4,5

Rather, as servants of God we commend ourselves in every way: in great endurance; in troubles, hardships and distresses.

In purity, understanding, patience and kindness; in the Holy Spirit and in sincere love.

2 Corinthians 6:4,6

Let us not become weary in doing good, for at the proper time we will reap a harvest if we do not give up.

Galatians 6:9

As a prisoner for the Lord, then, I urge you to live a life worthy of the calling you have received.

Ephesians 4:1

And we pray this in order that you may live a life worthy of the Lord and may please him in every way: bearing fruit in every good work, growing in the knowledge of God, being strengthened with all power according to his glorious might so that you may have great endurance and patience, and joyfully giving thanks to the Father, who has qualified you to share in the inheritance of the saints in the kingdom of light.

Colossians 1:10-12

Therefore, as God's chosen people, holy and dearly loved, clothe yourselves with compassion, kindness, humility, gentleness and patience.

Bear with each other and forgive whatever grievances you may have against one another. Forgive as the Lord forgave you.

Colossians 3:12,13

And we urge you, brothers, warn those who are idle, encourage the timid, help the weak, be patient with everyone.

1 Thessalonians 5:14

But you, man of God, flee from all this, and pursue righteousness, godliness, faith, love, endurance and gentleness.

1 Timothy 6:11

You need to persevere so that when you have done the will of God, you will receive what he has promised.

Hebrews 10:36

Be patient, then, brothers, until the Lord's coming. See how the farmer waits for the land to yield its valuable crop and how patient he is for the autumn and spring rains.

You too, be patient and stand firm, because the Lord's coming is near.

James 5:7,8

When a Customer Berates or Offends You

Do not seek revenge or bear a grudge against one of your people, but love your neighbor as yourself. I am the LORD.

Leviticus 19:18

O LORD my God, I take refuge in you; save and deliver me from all who pursue me.

Psalm 7:1

Those who know your name will trust in you, for you, LORD, have never forsaken those who seek you.

Psalm 9:10

To you, O LORD, I lift up my soul; in you I trust, O my God. Do not let me be put to shame, nor let my enemies triumph over me.

Psalm 25:1,2

Trust in the LORD and do good; dwell in the land and enjoy safe pasture.

Delight yourself in the LORD and he will give you the desires of your heart.

Commit your way to the LORD; trust in him and he will do this:

He will make your righteousness shine like the dawn, the justice of your cause like the noonday sun.

Refrain from anger and turn from wrath; do not fret — it leads only to evil.

Psalm 37:3-6,8

"Because he loves me," says the LORD, "I will rescue him; I will protect him, for he acknowledges my name.

He will call upon me, and I will answer him; I will be with him in trouble, I will deliver him and honor him."

Psalm 91:14,15

For the LORD will not reject his people; he will never forsake his inheritance.

Psalm 94:14

Do not say, "I'll pay you back for this wrong!" Wait for the LORD, and he will deliver you.

Proverbs 20:22

For if you forgive men when they sin against you, your heavenly Father will also forgive you.

Matthew 6:14

If he sins against you seven times in a day, and seven times comes back to you and says, "I repent," forgive him.

Luke 17:4

Do not repay anyone evil for evil. Be careful to do what is right in the eyes of everybody.

Romans 12:17

Love is patient, love is kind. It does not envy, it does not boast, it is not proud.

1 Corinthians 13:4

And the Lord's servant must not quarrel; instead, he must be kind to everyone, able to teach, not resentful.

2 Timothy 2:24

But the Lord stood at my side and gave me strength, so that through me the message might be fully proclaimed and all the Gentiles might hear it. And I was delivered from the lion's mouth.
The Lord will rescue me from every evil attack and will bring me safely to his heavenly kingdom. To him be glory for ever and ever. Amen.

2 Timothy 4:17,18

When a Customer Does Not Pay His Bills

I will instruct you and teach you in the way you should go; I will counsel you and watch over you.

Psalm 32:8

Teach me knowledge and good judgment, for I believe in your commands.

Psalm 119:66

Blessed is the man who finds wisdom, the man who gains understanding, for she is more profitable than silver and yields better returns than gold.
Have no fear of sudden disaster or of the ruin that overtakes the wicked, for the LORD will be your confidence and will keep your foot from being snared.

Proverbs 3:13,14,25,26

She is a tree of life to those who embrace her; those who lay hold of her will be blessed.

Proverbs 3:18

Stern discipline awaits him who leaves the path. He who hates correction will die.

Proverbs 15:10,12

A rebuke impresses a man of discernment more than a hundred lashes a fool.

Proverbs 17:10

When a mocker is punished, the simple gain wisdom; when a wise man is instructed, he gets knowledge.

Proverbs 21:11

He who rebukes a man will in the end gain more favor than he who has a flattering tongue.

Proverbs 28:23

If your brother sins against you, go and show him his fault, just between the two of you. If he listens to you, you have won your brother over.

Matthew 18:15

So watch yourselves. If your brother sins, rebuke him, and if he repents, forgive him.

Luke 17:3

Be joyful in hope, patient in affliction, faithful in prayer.

Romans 12:12

And we urge you, brothers, warn those who are idle, encourage the timid, help the weak, be patient with everyone.

1 Thessalonians 5:14

If any of you lacks wisdom, he should ask God, who gives generously to all without finding fault, and it will be given to him.

James 1:5

When a Customer Becomes a Nuisance

A patient man has great understanding, but a quick-tempered man displays folly.

Proverbs 14:29

A gentle answer turns away wrath, but a harsh word stirs up anger.

Proverbs 15:1

Better a patient man than a warrior, a man who controls his temper than one who takes a city.

Proverbs 16:32

A man's wisdom gives him patience; it is to his glory to overlook an offense.

Proverbs 19:11

It is to a man's honor to avoid strife, but every fool is quick to quarrel.

Proverbs 20:3

The end of a matter is better than its beginning, and patience is better than pride.

Ecclesiastes 7:8

If a ruler's anger rises against you, do not leave your post; calmness can lay great errors to rest.

Ecclesiastes 10:4

Blessed are the meek, for they will inherit the earth.

Blessed are the peacemakers, for they will be called sons of God.

Matthew 5:5,9

Bless those who persecute you; bless and do not curse.

If it is possible, as far as it depends on you, live at peace with everyone.

Romans 12:14,18

Do not cause anyone to stumble, whether Jews, Greeks or the church of God.

1 Corinthians 10:32

Love is patient, love is kind. It does not envy, it does not boast, it is not proud.

It is not rude, it is not self-seeking, it is not easily angered, it keeps no record of wrongs.

Love does not delight in evil but rejoices with the truth.

It always protects, always trusts, always hopes, always perseveres.

1 Corinthians 13:4-7

And we urge you, brothers, warn those who are idle, encourage the timid, help the weak, be patient with everyone.

1 Thessalonians 5:14

And the Lord's servant must not quarrel; instead, he must be kind to everyone, able to teach, not resentful.

2 Timothy 2:24

To slander no one, to be peaceable and considerate, and to show true humility toward all men.

Titus 3:2

Make every effort to live in peace with all men and to be holy; without holiness no one will see the Lord.

Hebrews 12:14

Peacemakers who sow in peace raise a harvest of righteousness.

James 3:18

When a Customer Is Dishonest

Unless the LORD had given me help, I would soon have dwelt in the silence of death.

When I said, "My foot is slipping," your love, O LORD, supported me.

Psalm 94:17,18

For your name's sake, O LORD, preserve my life; in your righteousness, bring me out of trouble.

Psalm 143:11

Instruct a wise man and he will be wiser still; teach a righteous man and he will add to his learning.

Proverbs 9:9

Better is open rebuke than hidden love.
Proverbs 27:5

But love your enemies, do good to them, and lend to them without expecting to get anything back. Then your reward will be great, and you will be sons of the Most High, because he is kind to the ungrateful and wicked.

Luke 6:35

No temptation has seized you except what is common to man. And God is faithful; he will not let you be tempted beyond what you can bear. But when you are tempted, he will also provide a way out so that you can stand up under it.

1 Corinthians 10:13

I pray that out of his glorious riches he may strengthen you with power through his Spirit in your inner being.

Ephesians 3:16

Finally, be strong in the Lord and in his mighty power.

Ephesians 6:10

For I know that through your prayers and the help given by the Spirit of Jesus Christ, what has happened to me will turn out for my deliverance.
Philippians 1:19

I can do everything through him who gives me strength.

Philippians 4:13

Therefore, as God's chosen people, holy and dearly loved, clothe yourselves with compassion, kindness, humility, gentleness and patience.

Bear with each other and forgive whatever grievances you may have against one another. Forgive as the Lord forgave you.

And over all these virtues put on love, which binds them all together in perfect unity.

And whatever you do, whether in word or deed, do it all in the name of the Lord Jesus, giving thanks to God the Father through him.

Colossians 3:12-14,17

When a Customer Embarrasses You

Keep me as the apple of your eye; hide me in the shadow of your wings.

Psalm 17:8

For in the day of trouble he will keep me safe in his dwelling; he will hide me in the shelter of his tabernacle and set me high upon a rock.

Then my head will be exalted above the enemies who surround me; at his tabernacle will I sacrifice with shouts of joy; I will sing and make music to the LORD.

Psalm 27:5,6

You are my hiding place; you will protect me from trouble and surround me with songs of deliverance. Selah.

Psalm 32:7

Hide me from the conspiracy of the wicked, from that noisy crowd of evildoers.

Psalm 64:2

Do not hide your face from me when I am in distress. Turn your ear to me; when I call, answer me quickly.

Psalm 102:2

You are my refuge and my shield; I have put my hope in your word.

Psalm 119:114

Set a guard over my mouth, O LORD; keep watch over the door of my lips.

Psalm 141:3

Answer me quickly, O LORD; my spirit fails. Do not hide your face from me or I will be like those who go down to the pit.

Rescue me from my enemies, O LORD, for I hide myself in you.

Teach me to do your will, for you are my God; may your good Spirit lead me on level ground.

Psalm 143:7,9,10

He who guards his mouth and his tongue keeps himself from calamity.

Proverbs 21:23

A word aptly spoken is like apples of gold in settings of silver.

Proverbs 25:11

There is a time for everything, and a season for every activity under heaven:
A time to tear and a time to mend, a time to be silent and a time to speak.

Ecclesiastes 3:1,7

Go, my people, enter your rooms and shut the doors behind you; hide yourselves for a little while until his wrath has passed by.

Isaiah 26:20

For by your words you will be acquitted, and by your words you will be condemned.

Matthew 12:37

Bless those who curse you, pray for those who mistreat you.

Luke 6:28

Do not let any unwholesome talk come out of your mouths, but only what is helpful for building others up according to their needs, that it may benefit those who listen.

Ephesians 4:29

Let your conversation be always full of grace, seasoned with salt, so that you may know how to answer everyone.

Colossians 4:6

My dear brothers, take note of this: Everyone should be quick to listen, slow to speak and slow to become angry.

James 1:19

When Your Employee Disappoints You

In you I trust, O my God. Do not let me be put to shame, nor let my enemies triumph over me.
Psalm 25:2

Free me from the trap that is set for me, for you are my refuge.
Into your hands I commit my spirit; redeem me, O LORD, the God of truth.

Psalm 31:4,5

You are my hiding place; you will protect me from trouble and surround me with songs of deliverance. Selah.

Psalm 32:7

All my longings lie open before you, O Lord; my sighing is not hidden from you.

Psalm 38:9

Therefore we will not fear, though the earth give way and the mountains fall into the heart of the sea.
The LORD Almighty is with us; the God of Jacob is our fortress. Selah.

Psalm 46:2,7

Be my rock of refuge, to which I can always go; give the command to save me, for you are my rock and my fortress.

Psalm 71:3

Surely God is my salvation; I will trust and not be afraid. The LORD, the LORD, is my strength and my song; he has become my salvation.

Isaiah 12:2

But as for me, I watch in hope for the LORD, I wait for God my Savior; my God will hear me.

Do not gloat over me, my enemy! Though I have fallen, I will rise. Though I sit in darkness, the LORD will be my light.

Micah 7:7,8

Though the fig tree does not bud and there are no grapes on the vines, though the olive crop fails and the fields produce no food, though there are no sheep in the pen and no cattle in the stalls, yet I will rejoice in the LORD, I will be joyful in God my Savior.

The Sovereign LORD is my strength; he makes my feet like the feet of a deer, he enables me to go on the heights. For the director of music. On my stringed instruments.

Habakkuk 3:17-19

Therefore we do not lose heart. Though outwardly we are wasting away, yet inwardly we are being renewed day by day.

2 Corinthians 4:16

We live by faith, not by sight.
2 Corinthians 5:7

That is why I am suffering as I am. Yet I am not ashamed, because I know whom I have believed, and am convinced that he is able to guard what I have entrusted to him for that day.
2 Timothy 1:12

Therefore, strengthen your feeble arms and weak knees.

"Make level paths for your feet," so that the lame may not be disabled, but rather healed.

Make every effort to live in peace with all men and to be holy; without holiness no one will see the Lord.

See to it that no one misses the grace of God and that no bitter root grows up to cause trouble and defile many.
Hebrews 12:12-15

When Your Employee Cheats You

When evil men advance against me to devour my flesh, when my enemies and my foes attack me, they will stumble and fall.

I am still confident of this: I will see the goodness of the LORD in the land of the living.

Wait for the LORD; be strong and take heart and wait for the LORD.
Psalm 27:2,13,14

The LORD is my strength and my shield; my heart trusts in him, and I am helped. My heart leaps for joy and I will give thanks to him in song.

Psalm 28:7

Free me from the trap that is set for me, for you are my refuge.

My times are in your hands; deliver me from my enemies and from those who pursue me.

Let your face shine on your servant; save me in your unfailing love.

Psalm 31:4,15,16

They repay me evil for good and leave my soul forlorn.

Psalm 35:12

Even my close friend, whom I trusted, he who shared my bread, has lifted up his heel against me.

But you, O LORD, have mercy on me; raise me up, that I may repay them.

Psalm 41:9,10

Cast your cares on the LORD and he will sustain you; he will never let the righteous fall.

Psalm 55:22

When I am afraid, I will trust in you. In God I trust; I will not be afraid.

What can man do to me?

Psalm 56:3,11

But I will sing of your strength, in the morning I will sing of your love; for you are my fortress, my refuge in times of trouble.

O my Strength, I sing praise to you; you, O God, are my fortress, my loving God.

Psalm 59:16,17

In you, O LORD, I have taken refuge; let me never be put to shame.

May my accusers perish in shame; may those who want to harm me be covered with scorn and disgrace.

But as for me, I will always have hope; I will praise you more and more.

My mouth will tell of your righteousness, of your salvation all day long, though I know not its measure.

I will come and proclaim your mighty acts, O Sovereign LORD; I will proclaim your righteousness, yours alone.

Psalm 71:1,13-16

Do not answer a fool according to his folly, or you will be like him yourself.

Proverbs 26:4

So watch yourselves. If your brother sins, rebuke him, and if he repents, forgive him.

Luke 17:3

When Your Employee Makes a Costly Error

He who covers over an offense promotes love, but whoever repeats the matter separates close friends.

A friend loves at all times, and a brother is born for adversity.

Proverbs 17:9,17

A man's wisdom gives him patience; it is to his glory to overlook an offense.

Proverbs 19:11

Perfume and incense bring joy to the heart, and the pleasantness of one's friend springs from his earnest counsel.

Proverbs 27:9

Blessed are the merciful, for they will be shown mercy.

Matthew 5:7

Forgive us our debts, as we also have forgiven our debtors.

Matthew 6:12

Do not repay anyone evil for evil. Be careful to do what is right in the eyes of everybody.

Romans 12:17

Be kind and compassionate to one another, forgiving each other, just as in Christ God forgave you.

Ephesians 4:32

Therefore, as God's chosen people, holy and dearly loved, clothe yourselves with compassion, kindness, humility, gentleness and patience.

Bear with each other and forgive whatever grievances you may have against one another. Forgive as the Lord forgave you.

And over all these virtues put on love, which binds them all together in perfect unity.

Colossians 3:12-14

And let us consider how we may spur one another on toward love and good deeds.

Hebrews 10:24

Do not repay evil with evil or insult with insult, but with blessing, because to this you were called so that you may inherit a blessing.

1 Peter 3:9

Above all, love each other deeply, because love covers over a multitude of sins.

1 Peter 4:8

Dear children, let us not love with words or tongue but with actions and in truth.

1 John 3:18

When Your Employee Slanders You

Keep me as the apple of your eye; hide me in the shadow of your wings.

Psalm 17:8

For in the day of trouble he will keep me safe in his dwelling; he will hide me in the shelter of his tabernacle and set me high upon a rock.

Then my head will be exalted above the enemies who surround me; at his tabernacle will I sacrifice with shouts of joy; I will sing and make music to the LORD.

Psalm 27:5,6

You are my hiding place; you will protect me from trouble and surround me with songs of deliverance. Selah.

Psalm 32:7

Evening, morning and noon I cry out in distress, and he hears my voice.

He ransoms me unharmed from the battle waged against me, even though many oppose me.

God, who is enthroned forever, will hear them and afflict them — Selah — men who never change their ways and have no fear of God.

My companion attacks his friends; he violates his covenant.

His speech is smooth as butter, yet war is in his heart; his words are more soothing than oil, yet they are drawn swords.

Cast your cares on the LORD and he will sustain you; he will never let the righteous fall.

Psalm 55:17-22

Be merciful to me, O God, for men hotly pursue me; all day long they press their attack.

In God, whose word I praise, in God I trust; I will not be afraid. What can mortal man do to me?
Psalm 56:1,4

I am in the midst of lions; I lie among ravenous beasts — men whose teeth are spears and arrows, whose tongues are sharp swords.

Be exalted, O God, above the heavens; let your glory be over all the earth.

They spread a net for my feet — I was bowed down in distress. They dug a pit in my path — but they have fallen into it themselves. Selah.

My heart is steadfast, O God, my heart is steadfast; I will sing and make music.
Psalm 57:4-7

O my Strength, I watch for you; you, O God, are my fortress.
Psalm 59:9

Hide me from the conspiracy of the wicked, from that noisy crowd of evildoers.
Psalm 64:2

Whoever slanders his neighbor in secret, him will I put to silence; whoever has haughty eyes and a proud heart, him will I not endure.
Psalm 101:5

Do not hide your face from me when I am in distress. Turn your ear to me; when I call, answer me quickly.

Psalm 102:2

I have hidden your word in my heart that I might not sin against you.
Your word is a lamp to my feet and a light for my path.
You are my refuge and my shield; I have put my hope in your word.

Psalm 119:11,105,114

Set a guard over my mouth, O LORD; keep watch over the door of my lips.

Psalm 141:3

Answer me quickly, O LORD; my spirit fails. Do not hide your face from me or I will be like those who go down to the pit.
Rescue me from my enemies, O LORD, for I hide myself in you.
Teach me to do your will, for you are my God; may your good Spirit lead me on level ground.

Psalm 143:7,9,10

He who conceals his hatred has lying lips, and whoever spreads slander is a fool.

Proverbs 10:18

With his mouth the godless destroys his neighbor, but through knowledge the righteous escape.

Proverbs 11:9

He who guards his mouth and his tongue keeps himself from calamity.

Proverbs 21:23

A word aptly spoken is like apples of gold in settings of silver.

Proverbs 25:11

A time to tear and a time to mend, a time to be silent and a time to speak.

Ecclesiastes 3:7

For by your words you will be acquitted, and by your words you will be condemned.

Matthew 12:37

Do not let any unwholesome talk come out of your mouths, but only what is helpful for building others up according to their needs, that it may benefit those who listen.

And do not grieve the Holy Spirit of God, with whom you were sealed for the day of redemption.

Get rid of all bitterness, rage and anger, brawling and slander, along with every form of malice.

Ephesians 4:29-31

Let your conversation be always full of grace, seasoned with salt, so that you may know how to answer everyone.

Colossians 4:6

My dear brothers, take note of this: Everyone should be quick to listen, slow to speak and slow to become angry.

James 1:19

For, "Whoever would love life and see good days must keep his tongue from evil and his lips from deceitful speech."

1 Peter 3:10

When Your Employee Is Hurting

And you are to love those who are aliens, for you yourselves were aliens in Egypt.

Deuteronomy 10:19

The Sovereign LORD has given me an instructed tongue, to know the word that sustains the weary. He wakens me morning by morning, wakens my ear to listen like one being taught.

Isaiah 50:4

Is it not to share your food with the hungry and to provide the poor wanderer with shelter — when you see the naked, to clothe him, and not to turn away from your own flesh and blood?

Isaiah 58:7

So in everything, do to others what you would have them do to you, for this sums up the Law and the Prophets.

Matthew 7:12

And the second is like it: "Love your neighbor as yourself."

Matthew 22:39

Then the King will say to those on his right, "Come, you who are blessed by my Father; take your inheritance, the kingdom prepared for you since the creation of the world.

For I was hungry and you gave me something to eat, I was thirsty and you gave me something to drink, I was a stranger and you invited me in, I needed clothes and you clothed me, I was sick and you looked after me, I was in prison and you came to visit me."

Matthew 25:34-36

By this all men will know that you are my disciples, if you love one another.

John 13:35

In everything I did, I showed you that by this kind of hard work we must help the weak, remembering the words the Lord Jesus himself said: "It is more blessed to give than to receive."

Acts 20:35

Rejoice with those who rejoice; mourn with those who mourn.

Romans 12:15

We who are strong ought to bear with the failings of the weak and not to please ourselves.

Romans 15:1

Praise be to the God and Father of our Lord Jesus Christ, the Father of compassion and the God of all comfort, who comforts us in all our troubles, so that we can comfort those in any trouble with the comfort we ourselves have received from God.

For just as the sufferings of Christ flow over into our lives, so also through Christ our comfort overflows.

2 Corinthians 1:3-5

Carry each other's burdens, and in this way you will fulfill the law of Christ.

Galatians 6:2

Remember those in prison as if you were their fellow prisoners, and those who are mistreated as if you yourselves were suffering.

And do not forget to do good and to share with others, for with such sacrifices God is pleased.

Hebrews 13:3,16

If you really keep the royal law found in Scripture, "Love your neighbor as yourself," you are doing right.

James 2:8

Finally, all of you, live in harmony with one another; be sympathetic, love as brothers, be compassionate and humble.

1 Peter 3:8

When Your Employee Has a Personal Crisis

I sought the LORD, and he answered me; he delivered me from all my fears.

Psalm 34:4

Be still, and know that I am God; I will be exalted among the nations, I will be exalted in the earth.

Psalm 46:10

One thing God has spoken, two things have I heard: that you, O God, are strong.

Psalm 62:11

Do not withhold good from those who deserve it, when it is in your power to act.

Do not say to your neighbor, "Come back later; I'll give it tomorrow" — when you now have it with you.

Proverbs 3:27,28

You are the salt of the earth. But if the salt loses its saltiness, how can it be made salty again? It is no longer good for anything, except to be thrown out and trampled by men.

You are the light of the world. A city on a hill cannot be hidden.

Neither do people light a lamp and put it under a bowl. Instead they put it on its stand, and it gives light to everyone in the house.

In the same way, let your light shine before men, that they may see your good deeds and praise your Father in heaven.

Give to the one who asks you, and do not turn away from the one who wants to borrow from you.

Matthew 5:13-16,42

So don't be afraid; you are worth more than many sparrows.

Matthew 10:31

For I was hungry and you gave me something to eat, I was thirsty and you gave me something to drink, I was a stranger and you invited me in, I needed clothes and you clothed me, I was sick and you looked after me, I was in prison and you came to visit me.

Then the righteous will answer him, "Lord, when did we see you hungry and feed you, or thirsty and give you something to drink?

When did we see you a stranger and invite you in, or needing clothes and clothe you?

When did we see you sick or in prison and go to visit you?"

The King will reply, "I tell you the truth, whatever you did for one of the least of these brothers of mine, you did for me."

Matthew 25:35-40

By standing firm you will gain life.

Luke 21:19

I will not leave you as orphans; I will come to you.

John 14:18

Not only so, but we also rejoice in our sufferings, because we know that suffering produces perseverance; perseverance, character; and character, hope.

And hope does not disappoint us, because God has poured out his love into our hearts by the Holy Spirit, whom he has given us.

Romans 5:3-5

Carry each other's burdens, and in this way you will fulfill the law of Christ.

Galatians 6:2

God is not unjust; he will not forget your work and the love you have shown him as you have helped his people and continue to help them.

Hebrews 6:10

If you really keep the royal law found in Scripture, ''Love your neighbor as yourself,'' you are doing right.

James 2:8

If anyone has material possessions and sees his brother in need but has no pity on him, how can the love of God be in him?

Dear children, let us not love with words or tongue but with actions and in truth.

1 John 3:17,18

When Your Employee Needs Motivation or Incentive

The LORD will grant that the enemies who rise up against you will be defeated before you. They will come at you from one direction but flee from you in seven.

Deuteronomy 28:7

Be strong and courageous. Do not be afraid or terrified because of them, for the LORD your God goes with you; he will never leave you nor forsake you.

Deuteronomy 31:6

As for me, far be it from me that I should sin against the LORD by failing to pray for you. And I will teach you the way that is good and right.

1 Samuel 12:23

"Don't be afraid," the prophet answered. "Those who are with us are more than those who are with them."

2 Kings 6:16

Through you we push back our enemies; through your name we trample our foes.

Psalm 44:5

An offended brother is more unyielding than a fortified city, and disputes are like the barred gates of a citadel.

Proverbs 18:19

It is better to heed a wise man's rebuke than to listen to the song of fools.

Ecclesiastes 7:5

For I am the LORD, your God, who takes hold of your right hand and says to you, Do not fear; I will help you.

Isaiah 41:13

The Spirit of the Sovereign LORD is on me, because the LORD has anointed me to preach good news to the poor. He has sent me to bind up the brokenhearted, to proclaim freedom for the captives and release from darkness for the prisoners.

Isaiah 61:1

Those who are wise will shine like the brightness of the heavens, and those who lead many to righteousness, like the stars for ever and ever.
Daniel 12:3

Ask and it will be given to you; seek and you will find; knock and the door will be opened to you.
For everyone who asks receives; he who seeks finds; and to him who knocks, the door will be opened.

Matthew 7:7,8

Then you will know the truth, and the truth will set you free.
So if the Son sets you free, you will be free indeed.

John 8:32,36

I tell you the truth, anyone who has faith in me will do what I have been doing. He will do even greater things than these, because I am going to the Father.

John 14:12

But you will receive power when the Holy Spirit comes on you; and you will be my witnesses in Jerusalem, and in all Judea and Samaria, and to the ends of the earth.

Acts 1:8

The weapons we fight with are not the weapons of the world. On the contrary, they have divine power to demolish strongholds.

2 Corinthians 10:4

For it is light that makes everything visible. This is why it is said: "Wake up, O sleeper, rise from the dead, and Christ will shine on you."

Ephesians 5:14

I can do everything through him who gives me strength.

Philippians 4:13

Being strengthened with all power according to his glorious might so that you may have great endurance and patience, and joyfully giving thanks to the Father, who has qualified you to share in the inheritance of the saints in the kingdom of light.

Colossians 1:11,12

Be wise in the way you act toward outsiders; make the most of every opportunity.

Colossians 4:5

For this reason I remind you to fan into flame the gift of God, which is in you through the laying on of my hands.

2 Timothy 1:6

Now he had to go through Samaria.

Jacob's well was there, and Jesus, tired as he was from the journey, sat down by the well. It was about the sixth hour.

He told her, "Go, call your husband and come back."

"I have no husband," she replied. Jesus said to her, "You are right when you say you have no husband."

John 4:4,6,16,17

When Your Employee Faces Termination

The LORD turn his face toward you and give you peace.

Numbers 6:26

For the LORD your God is a merciful God; he will not abandon or destroy you or forget the covenant with your forefathers, which he confirmed to them by oath.

Deuteronomy 4:31

Be strong and courageous. Do not be afraid or terrified because of them, for the LORD your God goes with you; he will never leave you nor forsake you.

The LORD himself goes before you and will be with you; he will never leave you nor forsake you. Do not be afraid; do not be discouraged.

Deuteronomy 31:6,8

I am still confident of this: I will see the goodness of the LORD in the land of the living.

Wait for the LORD; be strong and take heart and wait for the LORD.

Psalm 27:13,14

Let your face shine on your servant; save me in your unfailing love.

Psalm 31:16

I was young and now I am old, yet I have never seen the righteous forsaken or their children begging bread.

Psalm 37:25

Therefore I tell you, do not worry about your life, what you will eat or drink; or about your body, what you will wear. Is not life more important than food, and the body more important than clothes?

Therefore do not worry about tomorrow, for tomorrow will worry about itself. Each day has enough trouble of its own.

Matthew 6:25,34

May the God of hope fill you with all joy and peace as you trust in him, so that you may overflow with hope by the power of the Holy Spirit.

Romans 15:13

No temptation has seized you except what is common to man. And God is faithful; he will not let you be tempted beyond what you can bear. But when you are tempted, he will also provide a way out so that you can stand up under it.

1 Corinthians 10:13

Finally, be strong in the Lord and in his mighty power.

Ephesians 6:10

I am not saying this because I am in need, for I have learned to be content whatever the circumstances.

I know what it is to be in need, and I know what it is to have plenty. I have learned the secret of being content in any and every situation, whether well fed or hungry, whether living in plenty or in want.

I can do everything through him who gives me strength.

And my God will meet all your needs according to his glorious riches in Christ Jesus.

Philippians 4:11-13,19

Never will I leave you; never will I forsake you.

Hebrews 13:5b

These have come so that your faith — of greater worth than gold, which perishes even though refined by fire — may be proved genuine and may result in praise, glory and honor when Jesus Christ is revealed.

1 Peter 1:7

Cast all your anxiety on him because he cares for you.

1 Peter 5:7

When You Lose a Key Employee

Do not consider it a hardship to set your servant free, because his service to you these six years has been worth twice as much as that of a hired hand. And the LORD your God will bless you in everything you do.

Deuteronomy 15:18

The eternal God is your refuge, and underneath are the everlasting arms. He will drive out your enemy before you, saying, "Destroy him!"

Deuteronomy 33:27

My heart says of you, "Seek his face!" Your face, LORD, I will seek.

Psalm 27:8

If the LORD delights in a man's way, he makes his steps firm.

Psalm 37:23

Be still, and know that I am God; I will be exalted among the nations, I will be exalted in the earth.

Psalm 46:10

And call upon me in the day of trouble; I will deliver you, and you will honor me.

Psalm 50:15

Cast your cares on the LORD and he will
sustain you; he will never let the righteous fall.
Psalm 55:22

My flesh and my heart may fail, but God is
the strength of my heart and my portion forever.
Psalm 73:26

When I said, "My foot is slipping," your love,
O LORD, supported me.
When anxiety was great within me, your
consolation brought joy to my soul.
Psalm 94:18,19

He heals the brokenhearted and binds up their
wounds.

Psalm 147:3

So do not fear, for I am with you; do not be
dismayed, for I am your God. I will strengthen you
and help you; I will uphold you with my righteous
right hand.
All who rage against you will surely be
ashamed and disgraced; those who oppose you will
be as nothing and perish.
Though you search for your enemies, you will
not find them. Those who wage war against you
will be as nothing at all.
For I am the LORD, your God, who takes hold
of your right hand and says to you, Do not fear;
I will help you.

Isaiah 41:10-13

By standing firm you will gain life.

Luke 21:19

I am not saying this because I am in need, for I have learned to be content whatever the circumstances.

I know what it is to be in need, and I know what it is to have plenty. I have learned the secret of being content in any and every situation, whether well fed or hungry, whether living in plenty or in want.

I can do everything through him who gives me strength.

Philippians 4:11-13

Endure hardship with us like a good soldier of Christ Jesus.

2 Timothy 2:3

When Your Partnership Is Threatened

Guide me in your truth and teach me, for you are God my Savior, and my hope is in you all day long.

My eyes are ever on the LORD, for only he will release my feet from the snare.

Psalm 25:5,15

Summon your power, O God; show us your strength, O God, as you have done before.

Psalm 68:28

Direct my footsteps according to your word; let no sin rule over me.

Psalm 119:133

Do not accuse a man for no reason — when he has done you no harm.

Proverbs 3:30

Pride only breeds quarrels, but wisdom is found in those who take advice.

Proverbs 13:10

A hot-tempered man stirs up dissension, but a patient man calms a quarrel.

Proverbs 15:18

A perverse man stirs up dissension, and a gossip separates close friends.

Proverbs 16:28

Drive out the mocker, and out goes strife; quarrels and insults are ended.

Proverbs 22:10

But those who hope in the LORD will renew their strength. They will soar on wings like eagles; they will run and not grow weary, they will walk and not be faint.

Isaiah 40:31

So do not fear, for I am with you; do not be dismayed, for I am your God. I will strengthen you and help you; I will uphold you with my righteous right hand.

All who rage against you will surely be ashamed and disgraced; those who oppose you will be as nothing and perish.

Isaiah 41:10,11

Blessed are the peacemakers, for they will be called sons of God.

Matthew 5:9

If your brother sins against you, go and show him his fault, just between the two of you. If he listens to you, you have won your brother over.

Matthew 18:15

If it is possible, as far as it depends on you, live at peace with everyone.

Romans 12:18

Let us therefore make every effort to do what leads to peace and to mutual edification.

Romans 14:19

To one there is given through the Spirit the message of wisdom, to another the message of knowledge by means of the same Spirit.

1 Corinthians 12:8

And without faith it is impossible to please God, because anyone who comes to him must believe that he exists and that he rewards those who earnestly seek him.

Hebrews 11:6

If any of you lacks wisdom, he should ask God, who gives generously to all without finding fault, and it will be given to him.

James 1:5

For where you have envy and selfish ambition, there you find disorder and every evil practice.

But the wisdom that comes from heaven is first of all pure; then peace-loving, considerate, submissive, full of mercy and good fruit, impartial and sincere.

Peacemakers who sow in peace raise a harvest of righteousness.

James 3:16-18

When Your Colleague Needs Your Support

A friend loves at all times, and a brother is born for adversity.

Proverbs 17:17

Perfume and incense bring joy to the heart, and the pleasantness of one's friend springs from his earnest counsel.

As iron sharpens iron, so one man sharpens another.

As water reflects a face, so a man's heart reflects the man.

Proverbs 27:9,17,19

Two are better than one, because they have a good return for their work:

If one falls down, his friend can help him up.
But pity the man who falls and has no one to help
him up!

Ecclesiastes 4:9,10

But those who hope in the LORD will renew
their strength. They will soar on wings like eagles;
they will run and not grow weary, they will walk
and not be faint.

Isaiah 40:31

So in everything, do to others what you would
have them do to you, for this sums up the Law and
the Prophets.

Matthew 7:12

A new command I give you: Love one another.
As I have loved you, so you must love one another.

John 13:34

In everything I did, I showed you that by this
kind of hard work we must help the weak,
remembering the words the Lord Jesus himself
said: "It is more blessed to give than to receive."

Acts 20:35

That is, that you and I may be mutually
encouraged by each other's faith.

Romans 1:12

So that by God's will I may come to you with
joy and together with you be refreshed.

Romans 15:32

By all this we are encouraged. In addition to our own encouragement, we were especially delighted to see how happy Titus was, because his spirit has been refreshed by all of you.

2 Corinthians 7:13

Carry each other's burdens, and in this way you will fulfill the law of Christ.

Therefore, as we have opportunity, let us do good to all people, especially to those who belong to the family of believers.

Galatians 6:2,10

Finally, all of you, live in harmony with one another; be sympathetic, love as brothers, be compassionate and humble.

1 Peter 3:8

Dear friends, since God so loved us, we also ought to love one another.

1 John 4:11

When You Are Deceived

For in the day of trouble he will keep me safe in his dwelling; he will hide me in the shelter of his tabernacle and set me high upon a rock.

Teach me your way, O LORD; lead me in a straight path because of my oppressors.

Wait for the LORD; be strong and take heart and wait for the LORD.

Psalm 27:5,11,14

Into your hands I commit my spirit; redeem me, LORD, the God of truth.

I hate those who cling to worthless idols; I trust in the LORD.

For I hear the slander of many; there is terror on every side; they conspire against me and plot to take my life.

My times are in your hands; deliver me from my enemies and from those who pursue me.

Let your face shine on your servant; save me in your unfailing love.

Psalm 31:5,6,13,15,16

The angel of the LORD encamps around those who fear him, and he delivers them.

Taste and see that the LORD is good; blessed is the man who takes refuge in him.

Psalm 34:7,8

Ruthless witnesses come forward; they question me on things I know nothing about.

They repay me evil for good and leave my soul forlorn.

Yet when they were ill, I put on sackcloth and humbled myself with fasting. When my prayers returned to me unanswered, I went about mourning as though for my friend or brother. I bowed my head in grief as though weeping for my mother.

But when I stumbled, they gathered in glee; attackers gathered against me when I was unaware. They slandered me without ceasing.

Let not those gloat over me who are my enemies without cause; let not those who hate me without reason maliciously wink the eye.

They do not speak peaceably, but devise false accusations against those who live quietly in the land.

O LORD, you have seen this; be not silent. Do not be far from me, O Lord.

Psalm 35:11-15,19,20,22

Vindicate me, O God, and plead my cause against an ungodly nation; rescue me from deceitful and wicked men.

Psalm 43:1

Confuse the wicked, O Lord, confound their speech, for I see violence and strife in the city.

If an enemy were insulting me, I could endure it; if a foe were raising himself against me, I could hide from him.

But it is you, a man like myself, my companion, my close friend.

Psalm 55:9,12,13

He alone is my rock and my salvation; he is my fortress, I will never be shaken.

Psalm 62:2

He will cover you with his feathers, and under his wings you will find refuge; his faithfulness will be your shield and rampart.

You will not fear the terror of night, nor the arrow that flies by day.

Psalm 91:4,5

I will set before my eyes no vile thing. The deeds of faithless men I hate; they will not cling to me.

No one who practices deceit will dwell in my house; no one who speaks falsely will stand in my presence.

Psalm 101:3,7

Trust in the LORD with all your heart and lean not on your own understanding; in all your ways acknowledge him, and he will make your paths straight.

Proverbs 3:5,6

There is deceit in the hearts of those who plot evil, but joy for those who promote peace.

Proverbs 12:20

A truthful witness does not deceive, but a false witness pours out lies.

Proverbs 14:5

Whoever gives heed to instruction prospers, and blessed is he who trusts in the LORD.

Proverbs 16:20

A wicked man puts up a bold front, but an upright man gives thought to his ways.

Proverbs 21:29

A greedy man stirs up dissension, but he who trusts in the LORD will prosper.

Proverbs 28:25

Fear of man will prove to be a snare, but whoever trusts in the LORD is kept safe.

Proverbs 29:25

Surely God is my salvation; I will trust and not be afraid. The LORD, the LORD, is my strength and my song; he has become my salvation.

Isaiah 12:2

You will keep in perfect peace him whose mind is steadfast, because he trusts in you.

Trust in the LORD forever, for the LORD, the LORD, is the Rock eternal.

Isaiah 26:3,4

O LORD, be gracious to us; we long for you. Be our strength every morning, our salvation in time of distress.

Isaiah 33:2

Because the Sovereign LORD helps me, I will not be disgraced. Therefore have I set my face like flint, and I know I will not be put to shame.

He who vindicates me is near. Who then will bring charges against me? Let us face each other! Who is my accuser? Let him confront me!

It is the Sovereign LORD who helps me. Who
is he that will condemn me? They will all wear out
like a garment; the moths will eat them up.
Isaiah 50:7-9

But I will rescue you on that day, declares the
LORD; you will not be handed over to those you
fear.

I will save you; you will not fall by the sword
but will escape with your life, because you trust
in me, declares the LORD.
Jeremiah 39:17,18

Do not trust a neighbor; put no confidence in
a friend. Even with her who lies in your embrace
be careful of your words.

For a son dishonors his father, a daughter rises
up against her mother, a daughter-in-law against
her mother-in-law — a man's enemies are the
members of his own household.

But as for me, I watch in hope for the LORD,
I wait for God my Savior; my God will hear me.

Do not gloat over me, my enemy! Though I
have fallen, I will rise. Though I sit in darkness,
the LORD will be my light.
Micah 7:5-8

Do not be deceived: God cannot be mocked.
A man reaps what he sows.
Galatians 6:7

Therefore each of you must put off falsehood and speak truthfully to his neighbor, for we are all members of one body.

"In your anger do not sin": Do not let the sun go down while you are still angry.

Get rid of all bitterness, rage and anger, brawling and slander, along with every form of malice.

Ephesians 4:25,26,31

See to it that no one misses the grace of God and that no bitter root grows up to cause trouble and defile many.

Hebrews 12:15

Keeping a clear conscience, so that those who speak maliciously against your good behavior in Christ may be ashamed of their slander.

1 Peter 3:16

Nothing impure will ever enter it, nor will anyone who does what is shameful or deceitful, but only those whose names are written in the Lamb's book of life.

Revelation 21:27

When You Feel Betrayed

Teach me your way, O LORD; lead me in a straight path because of my oppressors.

Wait for the LORD; be strong and take heart and wait for the LORD.

Psalm 27:11,14

For I hear the slander of many; there is terror on every side; they conspire against me and plot to take my life.

My times are in your hands; deliver me from my enemies and from those who pursue me.

Let your face shine on your servant; save me in your unfailing love.

Psalm 31:13,15,16

The angel of the LORD encamps around those who fear him, and he delivers them.

Taste and see that the LORD is good; blessed is the man who takes refuge in him.

Psalm 34:7,8

Ruthless witnesses come forward; they question me on things I know nothing about.

They repay me evil for good and leave my soul forlorn.

Yet when they were ill, I put on sackcloth and humbled myself with fasting. When my prayers returned to me unanswered, I went about mourning as though for my friend or brother.

I bowed my head in grief as though weeping for my mother.

But when I stumbled, they gathered in glee; attackers gathered against me when I was unaware. They slandered me without ceasing.

Let not those gloat over me who are my enemies without cause; let not those who hate me without reason maliciously wink the eye.

They do not speak peaceably, but devise false accusations against those who live quietly in the land.

O LORD, you have seen this; be not silent. Do not be far from me, O Lord.

Psalm 35:11-15,19,20,22

Even my close friend, whom I trusted, he who shared my bread, has lifted up his heel against me.

But you, O LORD, have mercy on me; raise me up, that I may repay them.

I know that you are pleased with me, for my enemy does not triumph over me.

Psalm 41:9-11

If an enemy were insulting me, I could endure it; if a foe were raising himself against me, I could hide from him.

But it is you, a man like myself, my companion, my close friend, with whom I once enjoyed sweet fellowship as we walked with the throng at the house of God.

Psalm 55:12-14

He will cover you with his feathers, and under his wings you will find refuge; his faithfulness will be your shield and rampart.

You will not fear the terror of night, nor the arrow that flies by day.

Psalm 91:4,5

I will set before my eyes no vile thing. The deeds of faithless men I hate; they will not cling to me.

No one who practices deceit will dwell in my house; no one who speaks falsely will stand in my presence.

Psalm 101:3,7

A truthful witness does not deceive, but a false witness pours out lies.

Proverbs 14:5

Because the Sovereign LORD helps me, I will not be disgraced. Therefore have I set my face like flint, and I know I will not be put to shame.

He who vindicates me is near. Who then will bring charges against me? Let us face each other! Who is my accuser? Let him confront me!

It is the Sovereign LORD who helps me. Who is he that will condemn me? They will all wear out like a garment; the moths will eat them up.

Isaiah 50:7-9

Do not gloat over me, my enemy! Though I have fallen, I will rise. Though I sit in darkness, the LORD will be my light.

Micah 7:8

Then one of the Twelve — the one called Judas Iscariot — went to the chief priests and asked, "What are you willing to give me if I hand him over to you?" So they counted out for him thirty silver coins.

From then on Judas watched for an opportunity to hand him over.

Then he returned to the disciples and said to them, "Are you still sleeping and resting? Look, the hour is near, and the Son of Man is betrayed into the hands of sinners."

Matthew 26:14-16,45

Get rid of all bitterness, rage and anger, brawling and slander, along with every form of malice.

Ephesians 4:31

But the Lord stood at my side and gave me strength, so that through me the message might be fully proclaimed and all the Gentiles might hear it. And I was delivered from the lion's mouth.

2 Timothy 4:17

Keeping a clear conscience, so that those who speak maliciously against your good behavior in Christ may be ashamed of their slander.

1 Peter 3:16

When You Are Jealous

Keep your tongue from evil and your lips from speaking lies.

Psalm 34:13

Do not fret because of evil men or be envious of those who do wrong.

Psalm 37:1

Do not envy a violent man or choose any of his ways.

Proverbs 3:31

Righteousness exalts a nation, but sin is a disgrace to any people.

Proverbs 14:34

The tongue has the power of life and death, and those who love it will eat its fruit.

Proverbs 18:21

Do not envy wicked men, do not desire their company.

Proverbs 24:1

Place me like a seal over your heart, like a seal on your arm; for love is as strong as death, its jealousy unyielding as the grave. It burns like blazing fire, like a mighty flame.

Song of Songs 8:6

Be perfect, therefore, as your heavenly Father is perfect.

Matthew 5:48

Do not judge, or you too will be judged.

Matthew 7:1

Let us behave decently, as in the daytime, not in orgies and drunkenness, not in sexual immorality and debauchery, not in dissension and jealousy.

Romans 13:13

You are still worldly. For since there is jealousy and quarreling among you, are you not worldly? Are you not acting like mere men?

1 Corinthians 3:3

Love is patient, love is kind. It does not envy, it does not boast, it is not proud.

1 Corinthians 13:4

Those who belong to Christ Jesus have crucified the sinful nature with its passions and desires.

Since we live by the Spirit, let us keep in step with the Spirit.

Let us not become conceited, provoking and envying each other.

Galatians 5:24-26

Do not let any unwholesome talk come out of your mouths, but only what is helpful for building others up according to their needs, that it may benefit those who listen.

Get rid of all bitterness, rage and anger, brawling and slander, along with every form of malice.

Ephesians 4:29,31

Therefore, rid yourselves of all malice and all deceit, hypocrisy, envy, and slander of every kind.

Like newborn babies, crave pure spiritual milk, so that by it you may grow up in your salvation.
1 Peter 2:1,2

Do not repay evil with evil or insult with insult, but with blessing, because to this you were called so that you may inherit a blessing.
For, "Whoever would love life and see good days must keep his tongue from evil and his lips from deceitful speech."
1 Peter 3:9,10

But you, dear friends, build yourselves up in your most holy faith and pray in the Holy Spirit.
Jude 1:20

When You Feel Used

Be strong and courageous. Do not be afraid or terrified because of them, for the LORD your God goes with you; he will never leave you nor forsake you.

Deuteronomy 31:6

Those who know your name will trust in you, for you, LORD, have never forsaken those who seek you.

Psalm 9:10

As for God, his way is perfect; the word of the LORD is flawless. He is a shield for all who take refuge in him.

Psalm 18:30

O LORD, the king rejoices in your strength. How great is his joy in the victories you give!
You have granted him the desire of his heart and have not withheld the request of his lips. Selah.
Psalm 20:1,2

A righteous man may have many troubles, but the LORD delivers him from them all.
Psalm 34:19

Why are you downcast, O my soul? Why so disturbed within me? Put your hope in God, for I will yet praise him, my Savior and my God.
Psalm 43:5

Find rest, O my soul, in God alone; my hope comes from him.
Psalm 62:5

"Because he loves me," says the LORD, "I will rescue him; I will protect him, for he acknowledges my name.
He will call upon me, and I will answer him; I will be with him in trouble, I will deliver him and honor him."
Psalm 91:14,15

I wait for the LORD, my soul waits, and in his word I put my hope.
Psalm 130:5

The eyes of all look to you, and you give them their food at the proper time.

You open your hand and satisfy the desires of every living thing.

Psalm 145:15,16

Trust in the LORD with all your heart and lean not on your own understanding; in all your ways acknowledge him, and he will make your paths straight.

Proverbs 3:5,6

Above all else, guard your heart, for it is the wellspring of life.

Proverbs 4:23

So do not fear, for I am with you; do not be dismayed, for I am your God. I will strengthen you and help you; I will uphold you with my righteous right hand.

Isaiah 41:10

Can a mother forget the baby at her breast and have no compassion on the child she has borne? Though she may forget, I will not forget you!
See, I have engraved you on the palms of my hands; your walls are ever before me.

Isaiah 49:15,16

And teaching them to obey everything I have commanded you. And surely I am with you always, to the very end of the age.

Matthew 28:20

I have given you authority to trample on snakes and scorpions and to overcome all the power of the enemy; nothing will harm you.

Luke 10:19

What, then, shall we say in response to this? If God is for us, who can be against us?

Romans 8:31

So we say with confidence, ''The Lord is my helper; I will not be afraid. What can man do to me?''

Hebrews 13:6

Cast all your anxiety on him because he cares for you.

1 Peter 5:7

They overcame him by the blood of the Lamb and by the word of their testimony; they did not love their lives so much as to shrink from death.

Revelation 12:11

When You Face Illegal or Unfair Competition

Trust in the LORD and do good; dwell in the land and enjoy safe pasture.

Delight yourself in the LORD and he will give you the desires of your heart.

Commit your way to the LORD; trust in him and he will do this:

He will make your righteousness shine like the dawn, the justice of your cause like the noonday sun.

For evil men will be cut off, but those who hope in the LORD will inherit the land.

Psalm 37:3-6,9

A man's wisdom gives him patience; it is to his glory to overlook an offense.

Proverbs 19:11

Like a city whose walls are broken down is a man who lacks self-control.

Proverbs 25:28

The end of a matter is better than its beginning, and patience is better than pride. Do not be quickly provoked in your spirit, for anger resides in the lap of fools.

Ecclesiastes 7:8,9

Do to others as you would have them do to you.

Luke 6:31

By standing firm you will gain life.

Luke 21:19

To those who by persistence in doing good seek glory, honor and immortality, he will give eternal life.

Romans 2:7

Let us not become weary in doing good, for at the proper time we will reap a harvest if we do not give up.

Galatians 6:9

Do not be anxious about anything, but in everything, by prayer and petition, with thanksgiving, present your requests to God.

Finally, brothers, whatever is true, whatever is noble, whatever is right, whatever is pure, whatever is lovely, whatever is admirable — if anything is excellent or praiseworthy — think about such things.

Philippians 4:6,8

Make it your ambition to lead a quiet life, to mind your own business and to work with your hands, just as we told you, so that your daily life may win the respect of outsiders and so that you will not be dependent on anybody.

1 Thessalonians 4:11,12

And the Lord's servant must not quarrel; instead, he must be kind to everyone, able to teach, not resentful.

Those who oppose him he must gently instruct, in the hope that God will grant them repentance leading them to a knowledge of the truth.

2 Timothy 2:24,25

Because you know that the testing of your faith develops perseverance.

Perseverance must finish its work so that you may be mature and complete, not lacking anything.

He chose to give us birth through the word of truth, that we might be a kind of firstfruits of all he created.

James 1:3,4,18

For it is commendable if a man bears up under the pain of unjust suffering because he is conscious of God.

1 Peter 2:19

When You Are Asked To Participate in Unscrupulous Business Activities

For the LORD your God detests anyone who does these things, anyone who deals dishonestly.

Deuteronomy 25:16

I will maintain my righteousness and never let go of it; my conscience will not reproach me as long as I live.

Job 27:6

Who lends his money without usury and does not accept a bribe against the innocent. He who does these things will never be shaken.

Psalm 15:5

He who has clean hands and a pure heart, who does not lift up his soul to an idol or swear by what is false.

Psalm 24:4

The LORD abhors dishonest scales, but accurate weights are his delight.
The integrity of the upright guides them, but the unfaithful are destroyed by their duplicity.

Proverbs 11:1,3

The LORD detests lying lips, but he delights in men who are truthful.

Proverbs 12:22

He who walks righteously and speaks what is right, who rejects gain from extortion and keeps his hand from accepting bribes, who stops his ears against plots of murder and shuts his eyes against contemplating evil — this is the man who will dwell on the heights, whose refuge will be the mountain fortress. His bread will be supplied, and water will not fail him.

Isaiah 33:15,16

Tax collectors also came to be baptized. "Teacher," they asked, "what should we do?" "Don't collect any more than you are required to," he told them.

Luke 3:12,13

Do to others as you would have them do to you.

Luke 6:31

So I strive always to keep my conscience clear before God and man.

Acts 24:16

Rather, we have renounced secret and shameful ways; we do not use deception, nor do we distort the word of God. On the contrary, by setting forth the truth plainly we commend ourselves to every man's conscience in the sight of God.

2 Corinthians 4:2

Make room for us in your hearts. We have wronged no one, we have corrupted no one, we have exploited no one.

2 Corinthians 7:2

For we are taking pains to do what is right, not only in the eyes of the Lord but also in the eyes of men.

2 Corinthians 8:21

Pray for us. We are sure that we have a clear conscience and desire to live honorably in every way.

Hebrews 13:18

Live such good lives among the pagans that, though they accuse you of doing wrong, they may see your good deeds and glorify God on the day he visits us.

1 Peter 2:12

When Your Business Is Failing

But if from there you seek the LORD your God, you will find him if you look for him with all your heart and with all your soul.

When you are in distress and all these things have happened to you, then in later days you will return to the LORD your God and obey him.

Deuteronomy 4:29,30

Be strong and courageous. Do not be afraid or terrified because of them, for the LORD your God goes with you; he will never leave you nor forsake you.

Deuteronomy 31:6

Do not let this Book of the Law depart from your mouth; meditate on it day and night, so that you may be careful to do everything written in it. Then you will be prosperous and successful.

Have I not commanded you? Be strong and courageous. Do not be terrified; do not be discouraged, for the LORD your God will be with you wherever you go.

Joshua 1:8,9

David also said to Solomon his son, "Be strong and courageous, and do the work. Do not be afraid or discouraged, for the LORD God, my God, is with you. He will not fail you or forsake you until all the work for the service of the temple of the LORD is finished."

1 Chronicles 28:20

Teach me your way, O LORD; lead me in a straight path because of my oppressors.

Psalm 27:11

Since you are my rock and my fortress, for the sake of your name lead and guide me.

Psalm 31:3

For with you is the fountain of life; in your light we see light.

Psalm 36:9

When I am afraid, I will trust in you. In God, whose word I praise, in God I trust; I will not be afraid. What can mortal man do to me?

Psalm 56:3,4

Even in darkness light dawns for the upright, for the gracious and compassionate and righteous man. He will have no fear of bad news; his heart is steadfast, trusting in the LORD.

Psalm 112:4,7

It is better to take refuge in the LORD than to trust in man.

Psalm 118:8

Your word is a lamp to my feet and a light for my path.

Psalm 119:105

Trust in the LORD with all your heart and lean not on your own understanding.

Proverbs 3:5

The name of the LORD is a strong tower; the righteous run to it and are safe.

Proverbs 18:10

No, in all these things we are more than conquerors through him who loved us.

Romans 8:37

I can do everything through him who gives me strength.

Philippians 4:13

When You Face Litigation

But it is the spirit in a man, the breath of the Almighty, that gives him understanding.

Job 32:8

I will praise the LORD, who counsels me; even at night my heart instructs me.

Psalm 16:7

The LORD confides in those who fear him; he makes his covenant known to them.

Psalm 25:14

I will instruct you and teach you in the way you should go; I will counsel you and watch over you.

Psalm 32:8

Commit your way to the LORD; trust in him and he will do this:

He will make your righteousness shine like the dawn, the justice of your cause like the noonday sun.

Be still before the LORD and wait patiently for him; do not fret when men succeed in their ways, when they carry out their wicked schemes.

Refrain from anger and turn from wrath; do not fret — it leads only to evil.

Psalm 37:5-8

Surely you desire truth in the inner parts; you teach me wisdom in the inmost place.

Psalm 51:6

Even in darkness light dawns for the upright, for the gracious and compassionate and righteous man.

Psalm 112:4

He holds victory in store for the upright, he is a shield to those whose walk is blameless.

Proverbs 2:7

Trust in the LORD with all your heart and lean not on your own understanding; in all your ways acknowledge him, and he will make your paths straight.

Proverbs 3:5,6

Whether you turn to the right or to the left, your ears will hear a voice behind you, saying, "This is the way; walk in it."

Isaiah 30:21

Do not fear, for I am with you; do not be dismayed, for I am your God. I will strengthen you and help you; I will uphold you with my righteous right hand.

Isaiah 41:10

I will lead the blind by ways they have not known, along unfamiliar paths I will guide them; I will turn the darkness into light before them and make the rough places smooth. These are the things I will do; I will not forsake them.

Isaiah 42:16

This is what the LORD says — your Redeemer, the Holy One of Israel: "I am the LORD your God, who teaches you what is best for you, who directs you in the way you should go."

Isaiah 48:17

I thank and praise you, O God of my fathers: You have given me wisdom and power, you have made known to me what we asked of you, you have made known to us the dream of the king.

Daniel 2:23

When you are brought before synagogues, rulers and authorities, do not worry about how you will defend yourselves or what you will say, for the Holy Spirit will teach you at that time what you should say.

Luke 12:11,12

For I will give you words and wisdom that none of your adversaries will be able to resist or contradict.

Luke 21:15

But when he, the Spirit of truth, comes, he will guide you into all truth. He will not speak on his own; he will speak only what he hears, and he will tell you what is yet to come.

He will bring glory to me by taking from what is mine and making it known to you.

John 16:13,14

For God did not give us a spirit of timidity, but a spirit of power, of love and of self-discipline.

2 Timothy 1:7

When You Face a Hostile Board

You prepare a table before me in the presence of my enemies. You anoint my head with oil; my cup overflows.

Psalm 23:5

Since you are my rock and my fortress, for the sake of your name lead and guide me.

Free me from the trap that is set for me, for you are my refuge.

Into your hands I commit my spirit; redeem me, O LORD, the God of truth.

Psalm 31:3-5

You are my hiding place; you will protect me from trouble and surround me with songs of deliverance. Selah.

Psalm 32:7

Commit your way to the LORD; trust in him and he will do this:

He will make your righteousness shine like the dawn, the justice of your cause like the noonday sun.

Be still before the LORD and wait patiently for him; do not fret when men succeed in their ways, when they carry out their wicked schemes.

Psalm 37:5-7

I wait for you, O LORD; you will answer, O Lord my God.

Psalm 38:15

I said, "I will watch my ways and keep my tongue from sin; I will put a muzzle on my mouth as long as the wicked are in my presence."

Psalm 39:1

I call on the LORD in my distress, and he answers me.

Save me, O LORD, from lying lips and from deceitful tongues.

Psalm 120:1,2

Though I walk in the midst of trouble, you preserve my life; you stretch out your hand against the anger of my foes, with your right hand you save me.

Psalm 138:7

Set a guard over my mouth, O LORD; keep watch over the door of my lips.

Psalm 141:3

There are six things the LORD hates, seven that are detestable to him: haughty eyes, a lying tongue, hands that shed innocent blood, a heart that devises wicked schemes, feet that are quick to rush into evil, a false witness who pours out lies and a man who stirs up dissension among brothers.

Proverbs 6:16-19

The mouth of the righteous is a fountain of life, but violence overwhelms the mouth of the wicked.

Proverbs 10:11

Reckless words pierce like a sword, but the tongue of the wise brings healing.

Truthful lips endure forever, but a lying tongue lasts only a moment.

Proverbs 12:18,19

A gentle answer turns away wrath, but a harsh word stirs up anger.

The tongue of the wise commends knowledge, but the mouth of the fool gushes folly.

Proverbs 15:1,2

Commit to the LORD whatever you do, and your plans will succeed.

Pleasant words are a honeycomb, sweet to the soul and healing to the bones.

Proverbs 16:3,24

Do not say, "I'll do to him as he has done to me; I'll pay that man back for what he did."

Proverbs 24:29

When you pass through the waters, I will be with you; and when you pass through the rivers, they will not sweep over you. When you walk through the fire, you will not be burned; the flames will not set you ablaze.

Isaiah 43:2

The LORD will guide you always; he will satisfy your needs in a sun-scorched land and will strengthen your frame. You will be like a well-watered garden, like a spring whose waters never fail.

Isaiah 58:11

I the LORD search the heart and examine the mind, to reward a man according to his conduct, according to what his deeds deserve.

Jeremiah 17:10

The LORD is good, a refuge in times of trouble. He cares for those who trust in him.

Nahum 1:7

For by your words you will be acquitted, and by your words you will be condemned.

Matthew 12:37

"And when you stand praying, if you hold anything against anyone, forgive him, so that your Father in heaven may forgive you your sins."

They arrived again in Jerusalem, and while Jesus was walking in the temple courts, the chief priests, the teachers of the law and the elders came to him.

Mark 11:25,26

The good man brings good things out of the good stored up in his heart, and the evil man brings evil things out of the evil stored up in his heart. For out of the overflow of his heart his mouth speaks.

Luke 6:45

Do not let any unwholesome talk come out of your mouths, but only what is helpful for building others up according to their needs, that it may benefit those who listen.

Ephesians 4:29

Who is going to harm you if you are eager to do good?

1 Peter 3:13

Cast all your anxiety on him because he cares for you.

1 Peter 5:7

When You Have Made a Costly Mistake

But if from there you seek the LORD your God, you will find him if you look for him with all your heart and with all your soul.

When you are in distress and all these things have happened to you, then in later days you will return to the LORD your God and obey him.

For the LORD your God is a merciful God; he will not abandon or destroy you or forget the covenant with your forefathers, which he confirmed to them by oath.

Deuteronomy 4:29-31

Then the LORD your God will restore your fortunes and have compassion on you and gather you again from all the nations where he scattered you.

Deuteronomy 30:3

If my people, who are called by my name, will humble themselves and pray and seek my face and turn from their wicked ways, then will I hear from heaven and will forgive their sin and will heal their land.

2 Chronicles 7:14

If you put away the sin that is in your hand and allow no evil to dwell in your tent, then you will lift up your face without shame; you will stand firm and without fear.

Job 11:14,15

He restores my soul. He guides me in paths of righteousness for his name's sake.

Psalm 23:3

Wait for the LORD; be strong and take heart and wait for the LORD.

Psalm 27:14

Surely you desire truth in the inner parts; you teach me wisdom in the inmost place.

Create in me a pure heart, O God, and renew a steadfast spirit within me.

Do not cast me from your presence or take your Holy Spirit from me.

Restore to me the joy of your salvation and grant me a willing spirit, to sustain me.

Psalm 51:6,10-12

Cast your cares on the LORD and he will sustain you; he will never let the righteous fall.

Psalm 55:22

For the LORD will not reject his people; he will never forsake his inheritance.

Psalm 94:14

The LORD will fulfill for me; your love, O LORD, endures forever — do not abandon the works of your hands.

Psalm 138:8

The eyes of all look to you, and you give them their food at the proper time.

Psalm 145:15

He who conceals his sins does not prosper, but whoever confesses and renounces them finds mercy.

Proverbs 28:13

So do not fear, for I am with you; do not be dismayed, for I am your God. I will strengthen you and help you; I will uphold you with my righteous right hand.

Isaiah 41:10

I will repay you for the years the locusts have eaten — the great locust and the young locust, the other locusts and the locust swarm — my great army that I sent among you.

Joel 2:25

And we know that in all things God works for the good of those who love him, who have been called according to his purpose.

Romans 8:28

We live by faith, not by sight.

2 Corinthians 5:7

Brothers, if someone is caught in a sin, you who are spiritual should restore him gently. But watch yourself, or you also may be tempted.

Carry each other's burdens, and in this way you will fulfill the law of Christ.

Galatians 6:1,2

Brothers, I do not consider myself yet to have taken hold of it. But one thing I do: Forgetting what is behind and straining toward what is ahead, I press on toward the goal to win the prize for which God has called me heavenward in Christ Jesus.

Philippians 3:13,14

Let us hold unswervingly to the hope we profess, for he who promised is faithful.

Hebrews 10:23

Now faith is being sure of what we hope for and certain of what we do not see.

And without faith it is impossible to please God, because anyone who comes to him must believe that he exists and that he rewards those who earnestly seek him.

Hebrews 11:1,6

These have come so that your faith — of greater worth than gold, which perishes even though refined by fire — may be proved genuine and may result in praise, glory and honor when Jesus Christ is revealed.

1 Peter 1:7

But you are a chosen people, a royal priesthood, a holy nation, a people belonging to God, that you may declare the praises of him who called you out of darkness into his wonderful light.

1 Peter 2:9

Cast all your anxiety on him because he cares for you.

1 Peter 5:7

If we confess our sins, he is faithful and just and will forgive us our sins and purify us from all unrighteousness.

1 John 1:9

When Calamity Strikes

Be still, and know that I am God; I will be exalted among the nations, I will be exalted in the earth.

Psalm 46:10

One thing God has spoken, two things have I heard: that you, O God, are strong.

Psalm 62:11

My flesh and my heart may fail, but God is the strength of my heart and my portion forever.

Psalm 73:26

Though I walk in the midst of trouble, you preserve my life; you stretch out your hand against the anger of my foes, with your right hand you save me.

The LORD will fulfill for me; your love, O LORD, endures forever — do not abandon the works of your hands.

Psalm 138:7,8

Do not withhold good from those who deserve it, when it is in your power to act.

Do not say to your neighbor, "Come back later; I'll give it tomorrow" — when you now have it with you.

Proverbs 3:27,28

If you falter in times of trouble, how small is your strength!

Proverbs 24:10

You are the salt of the earth. But if the salt loses its saltiness, how can it be made salty again? It is no longer good for anything, except to be thrown out and trampled by men.

You are the light of the world. A city on a hill cannot be hidden.

Neither do people light a lamp and put it under a bowl. Instead they put it on its stand, and it gives light to everyone in the house.

In the same way, let your light shine before men, that they may see your good deeds and praise your Father in heaven.

Give to the one who asks you, and do not turn away from the one who wants to borrow from you.

Matthew 5:13-16,42

So don't be afraid; you are worth more than many sparrows.

Matthew 10:31

For I was hungry and you gave me something to eat, I was thirsty and you gave me something to drink, I was a stranger and you invited me in, I needed clothes and you clothed me, I was sick and you looked after me, I was in prison and you came to visit me.

Then the righteous will answer him, "Lord, when did we see you hungry and feed you, or thirsty and give you something to drink?

When did we see you a stranger and invite you in, or needing clothes and clothe you?

When did we see you sick or in prison and go to visit you?"

The King will reply, "I tell you the truth, whatever you did for one of the least of these brothers of mine, you did for me."

Matthew 25:35-40

By standing firm you will gain life.

Luke 21:19

I will not leave you as orphans; I will come to you.

John 14:18

Not only so, but we also rejoice in our sufferings, because we know that suffering produces perseverance; perseverance, character; and character, hope.

And hope does not disappoint us, because God has poured out his love into our hearts by the Holy Spirit, whom he has given us.

Romans 5:3-5

We are hard pressed on every side, but not crushed; perplexed, but not in despair; persecuted, but not abandoned; struck down, but not destroyed.

2 Corinthians 4:8,9

Carry each other's burdens, and in this way you will fulfill the law of Christ.

Galatians 6:2

God is not unjust; he will not forget your work and the love you have shown him as you have helped his people and continue to help them.

Hebrews 6:10

If you really keep the royal law found in Scripture, "Love your neighbor as yourself," you are doing right.

James 2:8

Dear friends, do not be surprised at the painful trial you are suffering, as though something strange were happening to you.

But rejoice that you participate in the sufferings of Christ, so that you may be overjoyed when his glory is revealed.

1 Peter 4:12,13

If anyone has material possessions and sees his brother in need but has no pity on him, how can the love of God be in him?

Dear children, let us not love with words or tongue but with actions and in truth.

1 John 3:17,18

When the Success of Your Business Depends on You Alone

Be strong and courageous. Do not be afraid or terrified because of them, for the LORD your God goes with you; he will never leave you nor forsake you.

Deuteronomy 31:6

But as for you, be strong and do not give up, for your work will be rewarded.

2 Chronicles 15:7

Be strong and take heart, all you who hope in the LORD.

Psalm 31:24

I will instruct you and teach you in the way you should go; I will counsel you and watch over you.

Psalm 32:8

You guide me with your counsel, and afterward you will take me into glory.

Psalm 73:24

Good will come to him who is generous and lends freely, who conducts his affairs with justice.

Psalm 112:5

For the LORD gives wisdom, and from his mouth come knowledge and understanding.

Proverbs 2:6

Trust in the LORD with all your heart and lean not on your own understanding.

Proverbs 3:5

Counsel and sound judgment are mine; I have understanding and power.

Proverbs 8:14

Do you see a man skilled in his work? He will serve before kings; he will not serve before obscure men.

Proverbs 22:29

Strengthen the feeble hands, steady the knees that give way.

Isaiah 35:3

So do not fear, for I am with you; do not be dismayed, for I am your God. I will strengthen you and help you; I will uphold you with my righteous right hand.

Isaiah 41:10

The Sovereign LORD is my strength; he makes my feet like the feet of a deer, he enables me to go on the heights. For the director of music. On my stringed instruments.

Habakkuk 3:19

But seek first his kingdom and his righteousness, and all these things will be given to you as well.

Matthew 6:33

But you will receive power when the Holy Spirit comes on you; and you will be my witnesses in Jerusalem, and in all Judea and Samaria, and to the ends of the earth.

Acts 1:8

To one there is given through the Spirit the message of wisdom, to another the message of knowledge by means of the same Spirit.

1 Corinthians 12:8

And God is able to make all grace abound to you, so that in all things at all times, having all that you need, you will abound in every good work.

2 Corinthians 9:8

Now to him who is able to do immeasurably more than all we ask or imagine, according to his power that is at work within us.

Ephesians 3:20

I can do everything through him who gives me strength.

Philippians 4:13

So do not throw away your confidence; it will be richly rewarded.

You need to persevere so that when you have done the will of God, you will receive what he has promised.

Hebrews 10:35,36

If any of you lacks wisdom, he should ask God, who gives generously to all without finding fault, and it will be given to him.

James 1:5

Your Daily Schedule

When You Feel Disorganized

Show me your ways, O LORD, teach me your paths.

Psalm 25:4

I will instruct you and teach you in the way you should go; I will counsel you and watch over you.

Psalm 32:8

Cast your cares on the LORD and he will sustain you; he will never let the righteous fall.

Psalm 55:22

Trust in the LORD with all your heart and lean not on your own understanding; in all your ways acknowledge him, and he will make your paths straight.

Proverbs 3:5,6

Make level paths for your feet and take only ways that are firm.

Proverbs 4:26

In his heart a man plans his course, but the LORD determines his steps.

Proverbs 16:9

Whether you turn to the right or to the left, your ears will hear a voice behind you, saying, "This is the way; walk in it."

Isaiah 30:21

He gives strength to the weary and increases the power of the weak.

Isaiah 40:29

When you pass through the waters, I will be with you; and when you pass through the rivers, they will not sweep over you. When you walk through the fire, you will not be burned; the flames will not set you ablaze.

Isaiah 43:2

Because the Sovereign LORD helps me, I will not be disgraced.

Isaiah 50:7a

I know, O LORD, that a man's life is not his own; it is not for man to direct his steps.

Jeremiah 10:23

Then, because so many people were coming and going that they did not even have a chance to eat, he said to them, "Come with me by yourselves to a quiet place and get some rest."

Mark 6:31

For God is not a God of disorder but of peace. As in all the congregations of the saints.

1 Corinthians 14:33

Therefore, my dear brothers, stand firm. Let nothing move you. Always give yourselves fully to the work of the Lord, because you know that your labor in the Lord is not in vain.

1 Corinthians 15:58

Let us not become weary in doing good, for at the proper time we will reap a harvest if we do not give up.

Galatians 6:9

Do not be anxious about anything, but in everything, by prayer and petition, with thanksgiving, present your requests to God.

And the peace of God, which transcends all understanding, will guard your hearts and your minds in Christ Jesus.

Philippians 4:6,7

For God did not give us a spirit of timidity, but a spirit of power, of love and of self-discipline.

2 Timothy 1:7

If any of you lacks wisdom, he should ask God, who gives generously to all without finding fault, and it will be given to him.

James 1:5

When Your Schedule Is Overbooked

The LORD is a refuge for the oppressed, a stronghold in times of trouble.

Psalm 9:9

A thousand may fall at your side, ten thousand at your right hand, but it will not come near you.

Then no harm will befall you, no disaster will come near your tent.

Psalm 91:7,10

Cast your cares on the LORD and he will sustain you; he will never let the righteous fall.

Psalm 55:22

Unless the LORD had given me help, I would soon have dwelt in the silence of death.

When I said, "My foot is slipping," your love, O LORD, supported me.

Psalm 94:17,18

Praise the LORD, O my soul, and forget not all his benefits.

He satisfies my desires with good things, so that your youth is renewed like the eagle's.

Psalm 103:2,5

Great peace have they who love your law, and nothing can make them stumble.

Psalm 119:165

For your name's sake, O LORD, preserve my life; in your righteousness, bring me out of trouble.

Psalm 143:11

When you lie down, you will not be afraid;
when you lie down, your sleep will be sweet.
Proverbs 3:24

Instruct a wise man and he will be wiser still;
teach a righteous man and he will add to his
learning.
Proverbs 9:9

The wicked are overthrown and are no more,
but the house of the righteous stands firm.
Proverbs 12:7

Better is open rebuke than hidden love.
Proverbs 27:5

But those who hope in the LORD will renew
their strength. They will soar on wings like eagles;
they will run and not grow weary, they will walk
and not be faint.
Isaiah 40:31

Because the Sovereign LORD helps me, I will
not be disgraced.
Isaiah 50:7a

No temptation has seized you except what is
common to man. And God is faithful; he will not
let you be tempted beyond what you can bear. But
when you are tempted, he will also provide a way
out so that you can stand up under it.
1 Corinthians 10:13

I pray that out of his glorious riches he may strengthen you with power through his Spirit in your inner being.

Ephesians 3:16

Finally, be strong in the Lord and in his mighty power.

Ephesians 6:10

Do not be anxious about anything, but in everything, by prayer and petition, with thanksgiving, present your requests to God.

And the peace of God, which transcends all understanding, will guard your hearts and your minds in Christ Jesus.

I can do everything through him who gives me strength.

Philippians 4:6,7,13

If any of you lacks wisdom, he should ask God, who gives generously to all without finding fault, and it will be given to him.

James 1:5

When Your Day Falls Apart

Do not cast me from your presence or take your Holy Spirit from me.

Restore to me the joy of your salvation and grant me a willing spirit, to sustain me.

Psalm 51:11,12

The Spirit of the LORD will rest on him — the Spirit of wisdom and of understanding, the Spirit of counsel and of power, the Spirit of knowledge and of the fear of the LORD.

Isaiah 11:2

For I will pour water on the thirsty land, and streams on the dry ground; I will pour out my Spirit on your offspring, and my blessing on your descendants.

They will spring up like grass in a meadow, like poplar trees by flowing streams.

Isaiah 44:3,4

I, even I, am he who comforts you. Who are you that you fear mortal men, the sons of men, who are but grass.

Isaiah 51:12

From the west, men will fear the name of the LORD, and from the rising of the sun, they will revere his glory. For he will come like a pent-up flood that the breath of the LORD drives along.

"As for me, this is my covenant with them," says the LORD. "My Spirit, who is on you, and my words that I have put in your mouth will not depart from your mouth, or from the mouths of your children, or from the mouths of their descendants from this time on and forever," says the LORD.

Isaiah 59:19,21

But as for me, I am filled with power, with the Spirit of the LORD, and with justice and might, to declare to Jacob his transgression, to Israel his sin.

Micah 3:8

But whoever drinks the water I give him will never thirst. Indeed, the water I give him will become in him a spring of water welling up to eternal life.

John 4:14

The Spirit gives life; the flesh counts for nothing. The words I have spoken to you are spirit and they are life.

John 6:63

The Spirit of truth. The world cannot accept him, because it neither sees him nor knows him. But you know him, for he lives with you and will be in you.

But the Counselor, the Holy Spirit, whom the Father will send in my name, will teach you all things and will remind you of everything I have said to you.

John 14:17,26

But when he, the Spirit of truth, comes, he will guide you into all truth. He will not speak on his own; he will speak only what he hears, and he will tell you what is yet to come.

John 16:13

In the same way, the Spirit helps us in our weakness. We do not know what we ought to pray for, but the Spirit himself intercedes for us with groans that words cannot express.

And he who searches our hearts knows the mind of the Spirit, because the Spirit intercedes for the saints in accordance with God's will.

Who shall separate us from the love of Christ? Shall trouble or hardship or persecution or famine or nakedness or danger or sword?

No, in all these things we are more than conquerors through him who loved us.

Romans 8:26,27,35,37

May the God of hope fill you with all joy and peace as you trust in him, so that you may overflow with hope by the power of the Holy Spirit.

Romans 15:13

Finally, be strong in the Lord and in his mighty power.

In addition to all this, take up the shield of faith, with which you can extinguish all the flaming arrows of the evil one.

And pray in the Spirit on all occasions with all kinds of prayers and requests. With this in mind, be alert and always keep on praying for all the saints.

Ephesians 6:10,16,18

But you, dear friends, build yourselves up in your most holy faith and pray in the Holy Spirit.

Jude 1:20

When You Face Constant Interruptions

It is God who arms me with strength and makes my way perfect.

He makes my feet like the feet of a deer; he enables me to stand on the heights.

2 Samuel 22:33,34

Look to the LORD and his strength; seek his face always.

1 Chronicles 16:11

The LORD is my rock, my fortress and my deliverer; my God is my rock, in whom I take refuge. He is my shield and the horn of my salvation, my stronghold.

To the faithful you show yourself faithful, to the blameless you show yourself blameless.

Psalm 18:2,25

A patient man has great understanding, but a quick-tempered man displays folly.

Proverbs 14:29

Better a patient man than a warrior, a man who controls his temper than one who takes a city.

Proverbs 16:32

The end of a matter is better than its beginning, and patience is better than pride.

Do not be quickly provoked in your spirit, for anger resides in the lap of fools.
Ecclesiastes 7:8,9

Give to the one who asks you, and do not turn away from the one who wants to borrow from you.
Matthew 5:42

Take my yoke upon you and learn from me, for I am gentle and humble in heart, and you will find rest for you souls.
Matthew 11:29

If it is possible, as far as it depends on you, live at peace with everyone.
Romans 12:18

Let us not become weary in doing good, for at the proper time we will reap a harvest if we do not give up.
Galatians 6:9

Being strengthened with all power according to his glorious might so that you may have great endurance and patience, and joyfully giving thanks to the Father, who has qualified you to share in the inheritance of the saints in the kingdom of light.
Colossians 1:11,12

Therefore, as God's chosen people, holy and dearly loved, clothe yourselves with compassion, kindness, humility, gentleness and patience.
Colossians 3:12

And we urge you, brothers, warn those who are idle, encourage the timid, help the weak, be patient with everyone.
1 Thessalonians 5:14

And the Lord's servant must not quarrel; instead, he must be kind to everyone, able to teach, not resentful.

2 Timothy 2:24

Because you know that the testing of your faith develops perseverance.

Perseverance must finish its work so that you may be mature and complete, not lacking anything.

My dear brothers, take note of this: Everyone should be quick to listen, slow to speak and slow to become angry.

James 1:3,4,19

When You Need a Break

Keep me as the apple of your eye; hide me in the shadow of your wings.

Psalm 17:8

He restores my soul. He guides me in paths of righteousness for his name's sake.

Psalm 23:3

For in the day of trouble he will keep me safe in his dwelling; he will hide me in the shelter of his tabernacle and set me high upon a rock.

Psalm 27:5

Be still before the LORD and wait patiently for him; do not fret when men succeed in their ways, when they carry out their wicked schemes.

Psalm 37:7

My heart pounds, my strength fails me; even the light has gone from my eyes.

For I am about to fall, and my pain is ever with me.

O LORD, do not forsake me; be not far from me, O my God.

Psalm 38:10,17,21

I said, ''Oh, that I had the wings of a dove! I would fly away and be at rest.''

Psalm 55:6

My flesh and my heart may fail, but God is the strength of my heart and my portion forever.

Psalm 73:26

Be at rest once more, O my soul, for the LORD has been good to you.

Psalm 116:7

Rescue me from my enemies, O LORD, for I hide myself in you.

For your name's sake, O LORD, preserve my life; in your righteousness, bring me out of trouble.

Psalm 143:9,11

Go, my people, enter your rooms and shut the doors behind you; hide yourselves for a little while until his wrath has passed by.

Isaiah 26:20

To whom he said, ''This is the resting place, let the weary rest''; and, ''This is the place of repose'' — but they would not listen.

Isaiah 28:12

My people will live in peaceful dwelling places, in secure homes, in undisturbed places of rest.

Isaiah 32:18

Come to me, all you who are weary and burdened, and I will give you rest.

Take my yoke upon you and learn from me, for I am gentle and humble in heart, and you will find rest for your souls.

Matthew 11:28,29

Then, because so many people were coming and going that they did not even have a chance to eat, he said to them, "Come with me by yourselves to a quiet place and get some rest."

So they went away by themselves in a boat to a solitary place.

Mark 6:31,32

There remains, then, a Sabbath-rest for the people of God.

Hebrews 4:9

Your Family

When You Face Marital Problems

The LORD God said, "It is not good for the man to be alone. I will make a helper suitable for him."

For this reason a man will leave his father and mother and be united to his wife, and they will become one flesh.

Genesis 2:18,24

The LORD is my light and my salvation — whom shall I fear? The LORD is the stronghold of my life — of whom shall I be afraid?

Psalm 27:1

Hatred stirs up dissension, but love covers over all wrongs.

Proverbs 10:12

So do not fear, for I am with you; do not be dismayed, for I am your God. I will strengthen you and help you; I will uphold you with my righteous right hand.

Isaiah 41:10

And provide for those who grieve in Zion — to bestow on them a crown of beauty instead of ashes, the oil of gladness instead of mourning, and a garment of praise instead of a spirit of despair. They will be called oaks of righteousness, a planting of the LORD for the display of his splendor.

They will rebuild the ancient ruins and restore the places long devastated; they will renew the ruined cities that have been devastated for generations.

Isaiah 61:3,4

For if you forgive men when they sin against you, your heavenly Father will also forgive you.

But if you do not forgive men their sins, your Father will not forgive your sins.

Matthew 6:14,15

Some Pharisees came and tested him by asking, "Is it lawful for a man to divorce his wife?"

"What did Moses command you?" he replied.

They said, "Moses permitted a man to write a certificate of divorce and send her away."

"It was because your hearts were hard that Moses wrote you this law," Jesus replied.

"But at the beginning of creation God 'made them male and female.'

Therefore what God has joined together, let man not separate."

Mark 10:2-6,9

Do not deprive each other except by mutual consent and for a time, so that you may devote yourselves to prayer. Then come together again so that Satan will not tempt you because of your lack of self-control.

To the married I give this command (not I, but the Lord): A wife must not separate from her husband.

1 Corinthians 7:5,10

Love is patient, love is kind. It does not envy, it does not boast, it is not proud.

It always protects, always trusts, always hopes, always perseveres.

1 Corinthians 13:4,7

Submit to one another out of reverence for Christ.

Wives, submit to your husbands as to the Lord.

Husbands, love your wives, just as Christ loved the church and gave himself up for her.

In this same way, husbands ought to love their wives as their own bodies. He who loves his wife loves himself.

However, each one of you also must love his wife as he loves himself, and the wife must respect her husband.

Ephesians 5:21,22,25,28,33

Wives, submit to your husbands, as is fitting in the Lord.

Husbands, love your wives and do not be harsh with them.

Colossians 3:18,19

When Your Spouse Is Unsupportive

The LORD is my light and my salvation — whom shall I fear? The LORD is the stronghold of my life — of whom shall I be afraid?

Though an army besiege me, my heart will not fear; though war break out against me, even then will I be confident.

Wait for the LORD; be strong and take heart and wait for the LORD.

Psalm 27:1,3,14

Since you are my rock and my fortress, for the sake of your name lead and guide me.

Free me from the trap that is set for me, for you are my refuge.

Psalm 31:3,4

You are my hiding place; you will protect me from trouble and surround me with songs of deliverance. Selah.

I will instruct you and teach you in the way you should go; I will counsel you and watch over you.

Psalm 32:7,8

My soul is weary with sorrow; strengthen me according to your word.

Psalm 119:28

Hatred stirs up dissension, but love covers over all wrongs.

Proverbs 10:12

A friend loves at all times, and a brother is born for adversity.

Proverbs 17:17

So in everything, do to others what you would have them do to you, for this sums up the Law and the Prophets.

Matthew 7:12

A new command I give you: Love one another. As I have loved you, so you must love one another.

John 13:34

I know what it is to be in need, and I know what it is to have plenty. I have learned the secret of being content in any and every situation, whether well fed or hungry, whether living in plenty or in want.

I can do everything through him who gives me strength.

And my God will meet all your needs according to his glorious riches in Christ Jesus.

Philippians 4:12,13,19

Bear with each other and forgive whatever grievances you may have against one another. Forgive as the Lord forgave you.

And over all these virtues put on love, which binds them all together in perfect unity.

Colossians 3:13,14

If any of you lacks wisdom, he should ask God, who gives generously to all without finding fault, and it will be given to him.

James 1:5

But if you harbor bitter envy and selfish ambition in your hearts, do not boast about it or deny the truth.

For where you have envy and selfish ambition, there you find disorder and every evil practice.

But the wisdom that comes from heaven is first of all pure; then peace-loving, considerate, submissive, full of mercy and good fruit, impartial and sincere.

Peacemakers who sow in peace raise a harvest of righteousness.

James 3:14,16-18

Therefore confess your sins to each other and pray for each other so that you may be healed. The prayer of a righteous man is powerful and effective.

James 5:16

When a Family Member Faces Sickness

The LORD will keep you free from every disease. He will not inflict on you the horrible diseases you knew in Egypt, but he will inflict them on all who hate you.

Deuteronomy 7:15

Praise the LORD, O my soul, and forget not all his benefits — who forgives all your sins and heals all your diseases.

Psalm 103:2,3

My son, pay attention to what I say; listen closely to my words.

Do not let them out of your sight, keep them within your heart; for they are life to those who find them and health to a man's whole body.

Proverbs 4:20-22

Surely he took up our infirmities and carried our sorrows, yet we considered him stricken by God, smitten by him, and afflicted.

But he was pierced for our transgressions, he was crushed for our iniquities; the punishment that brought us peace was upon him, and by his wounds we are healed.

Isaiah 53:4,5

Heal me, O LORD, and I will be healed; save me and I will be saved, for you are the one I praise.

Jeremiah 17:14

"But I will restore you to health and heal your wounds," declares the LORD.

Jeremiah 30:17a

Jesus said to him, "I will go and heal him."

Matthew 8:7

Jesus Christ is the same yesterday and today and forever.

Hebrews 13:8

Is any one of you in trouble? He should pray. Is anyone happy? Let him sing songs of praise.

Is any one of you sick? He should call the elders of the church to pray over him and anoint him with oil in the name of the Lord.

And the prayer offered in faith will make the sick person well; the Lord will raise him up. If he has sinned, he will be forgiven.

Therefore confess your sins to each other and pray for each other so that you may be healed. The prayer of a righteous man is powerful and effective.

James 5:13-16

Dear friend, I pray that you may enjoy good health and that all may go well with you, even as your soul is getting along well.

3 John 1:2

When Your Family Time Is Inadequate

Only be careful, and watch yourselves closely so that you do not forget the things your eyes have seen or let them slip from your heart as long as you live. Teach them to your children and to their children after them.

Deuteronomy 4:9

These commandments that I give you today are to be upon your hearts.

Impress them on your children. Talk about them when you sit at home and when you walk along the road, when you lie down and when you get up.

Deuteronomy 6:6,7

Fix these words of mine in your hearts and minds; tie them as symbols on your hands and bind them on your foreheads.

Teach them to your children, talking about them when you sit at home and when you walk along the road, when you lie down and when you get up.

Deuteronomy 11:18,19

He decreed statutes for Jacob and established the law in Israel, which he commanded our forefathers to teach their children.

Psalm 78:5

So the next generation would know them, even the children yet to be born, and they in turn would tell their children.

Then they would put their trust in God and would not forget his deeds but would keep his commands.

Psalm 78:6,7

Teach us to number our days aright, that we may gain a heart of wisdom.

Psalm 90:12

Blessed are all who fear the LORD, who walk in his ways.

You will eat the fruit of your labor; blessings and prosperity will be yours.

Your wife will be like a fruitful vine within your house; your sons will be like olive shoots around your table.

Thus is the man blessed who fears the LORD.

Psalm 128:1-4

In his heart a man plans his course, but the LORD determines his steps.

Proverbs 16:9

The righteous man leads a blameless life; blessed are his children after him.

Proverbs 20:7

Train a child in the way he should go, and when he is old he will not turn from it.

Proverbs 22:6

The father of a righteous man has great joy; he who has a wise son delights in him.

Proverbs 23:24

By wisdom a house is built, and through understanding it is established.

Proverbs 24:3

Discipline your son, and he will give you peace; he will bring delight to your soul.

Proverbs 29:17

He will be the sure foundation for your times, a rich store of salvation and wisdom and knowledge; the fear of the LORD is the key to this treasure.

Isaiah 33:6

All your sons will be taught by the LORD, and great will be your children's peace.

In righteousness you will be established: Tyranny will be far from you; you will have nothing to fear. Terror will be far removed; it will not come near you.

Isaiah 54:13,14

Tell it to your children, and let your children tell it to their children, and their children to the next generation.

Joel 1:3

But seek first his kingdom and his righteousness, and all these things will be given to you as well.

Matthew 6:33

What I mean, brothers, is that the time is short. From now on those who have wives should live as if they had none.

1 Corinthians 7:29

Be very careful, then, how you live — not as unwise but as wise, making the most of every opportunity, because the days are evil.

Ephesians 5:15,16

Fathers, do not exasperate your children; instead, bring them up in the training and instruction of the Lord.

Ephesians 6:4

Be wise in the way you act toward outsiders; make the most of every opportunity.

Colossians 4:5

He must manage his own family well and see that his children obey him with proper respect.
(If anyone does not know how to manage his own family, how can he take care of God's church?)

1 Timothy 3:4,5

If anyone does not provide for his relatives, and especially for his immediate family, he has denied the faith and is worse than an unbeliever.

1 Timothy 5:8

When Your Work Schedule Interferes With Your Church Life

If the LORD delights in a man's way, he makes his steps firm.

Psalms 37:23

Be still, and know that I am God; I will be exalted among the nations, I will be exalted in the earth.

Psalm 46:10

Cast your cares on the LORD and he will sustain you; he will never let the righteous fall.
Psalm 55:22

My flesh and my heart may fail, but God is the strength of my heart and my portion forever.
But as for me, it is good to be near God. I have made the Sovereign LORD my refuge; I will tell of all your deeds.

Psalm 73:26,28

The LORD is near to all who call on him, to all who call on him in truth.

Psalm 145:18

Seek the LORD while he may be found; call on him while he is near.

Isaiah 55:6

For the LORD will be your confidence.
Proverbs 3:26a

But those who hope in the LORD will renew their strength. They will soar on wings like eagles; they will run and not grow weary, they will walk and not be faint.

Isaiah 40:31

So do not fear, for I am with you; do not be dismayed, for I am your God. I will strengthen you and help you; I will uphold you with my righteous right hand.

Isaiah 41:10

Blessed are the merciful, for they will be shown mercy.

But I tell you: Love your enemies and pray for those who persecute you.

Matthew 5:7,44

But seek first his kingdom and his righteousness, and all these things will be given to you as well.

Matthew 6:33

Others, like seed sown on rocky places, hear the word and at once receive it with joy.

But since they have no root, they last only a short time. When trouble or persecution comes because of the word, they quickly fall away.

Still others, like seed sown among thorns, hear the word; but the worries of this life, the deceitfulness of wealth and the desires for other things come in and choke the word, making it unfruitful.

Mark 4:16-19

The seed that fell among thorns stands for those who hear, but as they go on their way they are choked by life's worries, riches and pleasures, and they do not mature.

Luke 8:14

Be careful, or your hearts will be weighed down with dissipation, drunkenness and the anxieties of life, and that day will close on you unexpectedly like a trap.

Luke 21:34

Do not neglect your gift, which was given you through a prophetic message when the body of elders laid their hands on you.

1 Timothy 4:14

How shall we escape if we ignore such a great salvation? This salvation, which was first announced by the Lord, was confirmed to us by those who heard him.

Hebrews 2:3

Let us hold unswervingly to the hope we profess, for he who promised is faithful.

Let us not give up meeting together, as some are in the habit of doing, but let us encourage one another — and all the more as you see the Day approaching.

Hebrews 10:23,25

Therefore, since we are surrounded by such a great cloud of witnesses, let us throw off everything that hinders and the sin that so easily entangles, and let us run with perseverance the race marked out for us.

Let us fix our eyes on Jesus, the author and perfecter of our faith, who for the joy set before him endured the cross, scorning its shame, and sat down at the right hand of the throne of God.

Hebrews 12:1,2

Come near to God and he will come near to you. Wash your hands, you sinners, and purify your hearts, you double-minded.

James 4:8

Your Finances

When It Seems Impossible To Pay Your Bills

The LORD is good, a refuge in times of trouble. He cares for those who trust in him.

Nahum 1:7

Since you are my rock and my fortress, for the sake of your name lead and guide me.

Psalm 31:3

I will instruct you and teach you in the way you should go; I will counsel you and watch over you.

Psalm 32:8

You guide me with your counsel, and afterward you will take me into glory.

Psalm 73:24

Good will come to him who is generous and lends freely, who conducts his affairs with justice.

Psalm 112:5

Though I walk in the midst of trouble, you preserve my life; you stretch out your hand against the anger of my foes, with your right hand you save me.

Psalm 138:7

For the LORD gives wisdom, and from his mouth come knowledge and understanding.

Proverbs 2:6

Trust in the LORD with all your heart and lean not on your own understanding.

Proverbs 3:5

Lazy hands make a man poor, but diligent hands bring wealth.

Proverbs 10:4

Diligent hands will rule, but laziness ends in slave labor.

Proverbs 12:24

The sluggard craves and gets nothing, but the desires of the diligent are fully satisfied.

Proverbs 13:4

Plans fail for lack of counsel, but with many advisers they succeed.

Proverbs 15:22

Do not love sleep or you will grow poor; stay awake and you will have food to spare.

Proverbs 20:13

Do you see a man skilled in his work? He will serve before kings; he will not serve before obscure men.

Proverbs 22:29

By wisdom a house is built, and through understanding it is established.

Proverbs 24:3

He who works his land will have abundant food, but the one who chases fantasies will have his fill of poverty.

Proverbs 28:19

Sow your seed in the morning, and at evening let not your hands be idle, for you do not know which will succeed, whether this or that, or whether both will do equally well.

Ecclesiastes 11:6

So do not fear, for I am with you; do not be dismayed, for I am your God. I will strengthen you and help you; I will uphold you with my righteous right hand.

Isaiah 41:10

But seek first his kingdom and his righteousness, and all these things will be given to you as well.

Matthew 6:33

Give, and it will be given to you. A good measure, pressed down, shaken together and running over, will be poured into your lap. For with the measure you use, it will be measured to you.

Luke 6:38

Never be lacking in zeal, but keep your spiritual fervor, serving the Lord.

Romans 12:11

Remember this: Whoever sows sparingly will also reap sparingly, and whoever sows generously will also reap generously.

2 Corinthians 9:6

And my God will meet all your needs according to his glorious riches in Christ Jesus.

Philippians 4:19

When You Need a Financial or Marketing Plan

God blessed them and said to them, ''Be fruitful and increase in number; fill the earth and subdue it. Rule over the fish of the sea and the birds of the air and over every living creature that moves on the ground.''

Genesis 1:28

But remember the LORD your God, for it is he who gives you the ability to produce wealth, and so confirms his covenant, which he swore to your forefathers, as it is today.

Deuteronomy 8:18

Carefully follow the terms of this covenant, so that you may prosper in everything you do.

Deuteronomy 29:9

Be strong and very courageous. Be careful to obey all the law my servant Moses gave you; do not turn from it to the right or to the left, that you may be successful wherever you go.

Do not let this Book of the Law depart from your mouth; meditate on it day and night, so that you may be careful to do everything written in it. Then you will be prosperous and successful.

Joshua 1:7,8

That night God appeared to Solomon and said to him, ''Ask for whatever you want me to give you.''

Solomon answered God, ''You have shown great kindness to David my father and have made me king in his place.

Now, LORD God, let your promise to my father David be confirmed, for you have made me king over a people who are as numerous as the dust of the earth.

Give me wisdom and knowledge, that I may lead this people, for who is able to govern this great people of yours?''

God said to Solomon, ''Since this is your heart's desire and you have not asked for wealth, riches or honor, nor for the death of your enemies, and since you have not asked for a long life but for wisdom and knowledge to govern my people over whom I have made you king, therefore wisdom and knowledge will be given you. And I will also give you wealth, riches and honor, such as no king who was before you ever had and none after you will have.''

2 Chronicles 1:7-12

Guide me in your truth and teach me, for you are God my Savior, and my hope is in you all day long.

He guides the humble in what is right and teaches them his way.

Who, then, is the man that fears the LORD? He will instruct him in the way chosen for him.

Psalm 25:5,9,12

Teach me your way, O LORD; lead me in a straight path because of my oppressors.

Psalm 27:11

Since you are my rock and my fortress, for the sake of your name lead and guide me.

Psalm 31:3

I will instruct you and teach you in the way you should go; I will counsel you and watch over you.

Psalm 32:8

You guide me with your counsel, and afterward you will take me into glory.

Psalm 73:24

If you had responded to my rebuke, I would have poured out my heart to you and made my thoughts known to you.

Proverbs 1:23

For the LORD gives wisdom, and from his mouth come knowledge and understanding.

Proverbs 2:6

I walk in the way of righteousness, along the paths of justice, bestowing wealth on those who love me and making their treasuries full.

Proverbs 8:20,21

Sow your seed in the morning, and at evening let not your hands be idle, for you do not know which will succeed, whether this or that, or whether both will do equally well.

Ecclesiastes 11:6

I will lead the blind by ways they have not known, along unfamiliar paths I will guide them; I will turn the darkness into light before them and make the rough places smooth. These are the things I will do; I will not forsake them.

Isaiah 42:16

The LORD will guide you always; he will satisfy your needs in a sun-scorched land and will strengthen your frame. You will be like a well-watered garden, like a spring whose waters never fail.

Isaiah 58:11

Call to me and I will answer you and tell you great and unsearchable things you do not know.
Jeremiah 33:3

To one there is given through the Spirit the message of wisdom, to another the message of knowledge by means of the same Spirit.
1 Corinthians 12:8

Dear friend, I pray that you may enjoy good health and that all may go well with you, even as your soul is getting along well.
3 John 1:2

When You Face a Volatile Economy

Have faith in the LORD your God and you will be upheld; have faith in his prophets and you will be successful.
2 Chronicles 20:20b

My soul finds rest in God alone; my salvation comes from him.
He alone is my rock and my salvation; he is my fortress, I will never be shaken.
Psalm 62:1,2

May the favor of the Lord our God rest upon us; establish the work of our hands for us — yes, establish the work of our hands.
Psalm 90:17

Good will come to him who is generous and lends freely, who conducts his affairs with justice.

Surely he will never be shaken; a righteous man will be remembered forever.

He will have no fear of bad news; his heart is steadfast, trusting in the LORD.

His heart is secure, he will have no fear; in the end he will look in triumph on his foes.

Psalm 112:5-8

I lift up my eyes to the hills — where does my help come from?

My help comes from the LORD, the Maker of heaven and earth.

He will not let your foot slip — he who watches over you will not slumber.

Psalm 121:1-3

Plans fail for lack of counsel, but with many advisors they succeed.

Proverbs 15:22

Commit to the LORD whatever you do, and your plans will succeed.

Proverbs 16:3

Make plans by seeking advice; if you wage war, obtain guidance.

Proverbs 20:18

You will keep in perfect peace him whose mind is steadfast, because he trusts in you.

Isaiah 26:3

So this is what the Sovereign LORD says: "See, I lay a stone in Zion, a tested stone, a precious cornerstone for a sure foundation; the one who trusts will never be dismayed."

Isaiah 28:16

So do not worry, saying, "What shall we eat?" or "What shall we drink?" or "What shall we wear?"

For the pagans run after all these things, and your heavenly Father knows that you need them.

But seek first his kingdom and his righteousness, and all these things will be given to you as well.

Matthew 6:31-33

I will show you what he is like who comes to me and hears my words and puts them into practice.

He is like a man building a house, who dug down deep and laid the foundation on rock. When a flood came, the torrent struck that house but could not shake it, because it was well built.

But the one who hears my words and does not put them into practice is like a man who built a house on the ground without a foundation. The moment the torrent struck that house, it collapsed and its destruction was complete.

Luke 6:47-49

So I say to you: Ask and it will be given to you; seek and you will find; knock and the door will be opened to you.

For everyone who asks receives; he who seeks finds; and to him who knocks, the door will be opened.

Luke 11:9,10

Do not conform any longer to the pattern of this world, but be transformed by the renewing of your mind. Then you will be able to test and approve what God's will is — his good, pleasing and perfect will.

Romans 12:2

When You Are Tempted To Cheat

Be careful that you do not forget the LORD your God, failing to observe his commands, his laws and his decrees that I am giving you this day.

But remember the LORD your God, for it is he who gives you the ability to produce wealth, and so confirms his covenant, which he swore to your forefathers, as it is today.

Deuteronomy 8:11,18

Unless the LORD had given me help, I would soon have dwelt in the silence of death.

When I said, "My foot is slipping," your love, O LORD, supported me.

Psalm 94:17,18

My son, if sinners entice you, do not give in to them. My son, do not go along with them, do not set foot on their paths.

Proverbs 1:10,15

Do not set foot on the path of the wicked or walk in the way of evil men.

Proverbs 4:14

He who walks righteously and speaks what is right, who rejects gain from extortion and keeps his hand from accepting bribes, who stops his ears against plots of murder and shuts his eyes against contemplating evil — this is the man who will dwell on the heights, whose refuge will be the mountain fortress. His bread will be supplied, and water will not fail him.

Isaiah 33:15,16

If your hand or your foot causes you to sin cut it off and throw it away. It is better for you to enter life maimed or crippled than to have two hands or two feet and be thrown into eternal fire.

And if your eye causes you to sin, gouge it out and throw it away. It is better for you to enter life with one eye than to have two eyes and be thrown into the fire of hell.

Matthew 18:8,9

Watch and pray so that you will not fall into temptation. The spirit is willing, but the body is weak.

Matthew 26:41

Forgive us our sins, for we also forgive everyone who sins against us. And lead us not into temptation.

Luke 11:4

Therefore do not let sin reign in your mortal body so that you obey its evil desires.

Do not offer the parts of your body to sin, as instruments of wickedness, but rather offer yourselves to God, as those who have been brought from death to life; and offer the parts of your body to him as instruments of righteousness.

Romans 6:12,13

Do not be overcome by evil, but overcome evil with good.

Romans 12:21

No temptation has seized you except what is common to man. And God is faithful; he will not let you be tempted beyond what you can bear. But when you are tempted, he will also provide a way out so that you can stand up under it.

1 Corinthians 10:13

Be on your guard; stand firm in the faith; be men of courage; be strong.

1 Corinthians 16:13

He who has been stealing must steal no longer,
but must work, doing something useful with his
own hands, that he may have something to share
with those in need.

Ephesians 4:28

When tempted, no one should say, "God is
tempting me." For God cannot be tempted by evil,
nor does he tempt anyone; but each one is tempted
when, by his own evil desire, he is dragged away
and enticed.

Then, after desire has conceived, it gives birth
to sin; and sin, when it is full-grown, gives birth
to death.

Don't be deceived, my dear brothers.

James 1:13-16

Submit yourselves, then, to God. Resist the
devil, and he will flee from you.

James 4:7

Be self-controlled and alert. Your enemy the
devil prowls around like a roaring lion looking for
someone to devour.

Resist him, standing firm in the faith, because
you know that your brothers throughout the world
are undergoing the same kind of sufferings.

1 Peter 5:8,9

When Tithing Seems Too Difficult

But as for you, be strong and do not give up,
for your work will be rewarded.

2 Chronicles 15:7

Make vows to the LORD your God and fulfill them; let all the neighboring lands bring gifts to the One to be feared.

Psalm 76:11

Good will come to him who is generous and lends freely, who conducts his affairs with justice.
He has scattered abroad his gifts to the poor, his righteousness endures forever; his horn will be lifted high in honor.

Psalm 112:5,9

Honor the LORD with your wealth, with the firstfruits of all your crops; then your barns will be filled to overflowing, and your vats will brim over with new wine.

Proverbs 3:9,10

Lazy hands make a man poor, but diligent hands bring wealth.

Proverbs 10:4

He who is kind to the poor lends to the LORD, and he will reward him for what he has done.

Proverbs 19:17

All day long he craves for more, but the righteous give without sparing.

Proverbs 21:26

A generous man will himself be blessed, for he shares his food with the poor.

Proverbs 22:9

He who gives to the poor will lack nothing, but he who closes his eyes to them receives many curses.

Proverbs 28:27

Cast your bread upon the waters, for after many days you will find it again.

Ecclesiastes 11:1

If you are willing and obedient, you will eat the best from the land.

Isaiah 1:19

"Bring the whole tithe into the storehouse, that there may be food in my house. Test me in this," says the LORD Almighty, "and see if I will not throw open the floodgates of heaven and pour out so much blessing that you will not have room enough for it.

I will prevent pests from devouring your crops, and the vines in your fields will not cast their fruit," says the LORD Almighty.

Malachi 3:10,11

Give to the one who asks you, and do not turn away from the one who wants to borrow from you.

Matthew 5:42

Give, and it will be given to you. A good measure, pressed down, shaken together and running over, will be poured into your lap. For with the measure you use, it will be measured to you.

Luke 6:38

On the first day of every week, each one of you should set aside a sum of money in keeping with his income, saving it up, so that when I come no collections will have to be made.

1 Corinthians 16:2

Remember this: Whoever sows sparingly will also reap sparingly, and whoever sows generously will also reap generously.

Each man should give what he has decided in his heart to give, not reluctantly or under compulsion, for God loves a cheerful giver.

And God is able to make all grace abound to you, so that in all things at all times, having all that you need, you will abound in every good work.

2 Corinthians 9:6-8

Command those who are rich in this present world not to be arrogant nor to put their hope in wealth, which is so uncertain, but to put their hope in God, who richly provides us with everything for our enjoyment.

Command them to do good, to be rich in good deeds, and to be generous and willing to share.

In this way they will lay up treasure for themselves as a firm foundation for the coming age, so that they may take hold of the life that is truly life.

1 Timothy 6:17-19

If anyone has material possessions and sees his brother in need but has no pity on him, how can the love of God be in him?

Dear children, let us not love with words or tongue but with actions and in truth.

1 John 3:17,18

When a Business Deal Falls Through

The LORD sends poverty and wealth; he humbles and he exalts.

He will guard the feet of his saints, but the wicked will be silenced in darkness. It is not by strength that one prevails.

1 Samuel 2:7,9

At least there is hope for a tree: If it is cut down, it will sprout again, and its new shoots will not fail.

Its roots may grow old in the ground and its stump die in the soil, yet at the scent of water it will bud and put forth shoots like a plant.

Job 14:7-9

But the needy will not always be forgotten, nor the hope of the afflicted ever perish.

Psalm 9:18

I will be glad and rejoice in your love, for you saw my affliction and knew the anguish of my soul.

Be strong and take heart, all you who hope in the LORD.

Psalm 31:7,24

Why are you downcast, O my soul? Why so disturbed within me? Put your hope in God, for I will yet praise him, my Savior and my God.

Psalm 43:5

But as for me, I will always have hope; I will praise you more and more.

Psalm 71:14

I will meditate on all your works and consider all your mighty deeds.

Your ways, O God, are holy. What god is so great as our God?

You are the God who performs miracles; you display your power among the peoples.

Psalm 77:12-14

The blessing of the LORD brings wealth, and he adds no trouble to it.

Proverbs 10:22

There is surely a future hope for you, and your hope will not be cut off.

Proverbs 23:18

If you falter in times of trouble, how small is your strength!

Proverbs 24:10

Finally, be strong in the Lord and in his mighty power.

Ephesians 6:10

I know what it is to be in need, and I know what it is to have plenty.

I have learned the secret of being content in any and every situation, whether well fed or hungry, whether living in plenty or in want. I can do everything through him who gives me strength.
Philippians 4:12,13

Let us then approach the throne of grace with confidence, so that we may receive mercy and find grace to help us in our time of need.
Hebrews 4:16

If any of you lacks wisdom, he should ask God, who gives generously to all without finding fault, and it will be given to him.
James 1:5

Your Personal Life

When You Are Overworked

I will lie down and sleep in peace, for you alone, O LORD, make me dwell in safety.

Psalm 4:8

He makes me lie down in green pastures, he leads me beside quiet waters, he restores my soul.

He guides me in paths of righteousness for his name's sake.

Psalm 23:2,3

My heart says of you, "Seek his face!" Your face, LORD, I will seek.

Psalm 27:8

The LORD gives strength to his people; the LORD blesses his people with peace.

Psalm 29:11

Delight yourself in the LORD and he will give you the desires of your heart.

Commit your way to the LORD; trust in him and he will do this:

He will make your righteousness shine like the dawn, the justice of your cause like the noonday sun.

Be still before the LORD and wait patiently for him; do not fret when men succeed in their ways, when they carry out their wicked schemes.

But the meek will inherit the land and enjoy great peace.

Psalm 37:4-7,11

My flesh and my heart may fail, but God is the strength of my heart and my portion forever.
Psalm 73:26

I will listen to what God the LORD will say; he promises peace to his people, his saints — but let them not return to folly.
Psalm 85:8

You will keep in perfect peace him whose mind is steadfast, because he trusts in you.
Isaiah 26:3

To whom he said, ''This is the resting place, let the weary rest''; and, ''This is the place of repose'' — but they would not listen.
Isaiah 28:12

This is what the Sovereign LORD, the Holy One of Israel, says: ''In repentance and rest is your salvation, in quietness and trust is your strength, but you would have none of it.''
Isaiah 30:15

Come to me, all you who are weary and burdened, and I will give you rest.
Take my yoke upon you and learn from me, for I am gentle and humble in heart, and you will find rest for your souls.
Matthew 11:28,29

Then, because so many people were coming and going that they did not even have a chance to eat, he said to them, "Come with me by yourselves to a quiet place and get some rest."

Mark 6:31

Peace I leave with you; my peace I give you. I do not give to you as the world gives. Do not let your hearts be troubled and do not be afraid.

John 14:27

Don't you know that you yourselves are God's temple and that God's Spirit lives in you?

If anyone destroys God's temple, God will destroy him; for God's temple is sacred, and you are that temple.

1 Corinthians 3:16,17

"Everything is permissible" — but not everything is beneficial. "Everything is permissible" — but not everything is constructive.

1 Corinthians 10:23

When You Are Under Stress

One of you routs a thousand, because the LORD your God fights for you, just as he promised.

Joshua 23:10

He will guard the feet of his saints, but the wicked will be silenced in darkness. It is not by strength that one prevails.

1 Samuel 2:9

This is what the LORD says to you: Do not be afraid or discouraged because of this vast army. For the battle is not yours, but God's.
2 Chronicles 20:15b

But you are a shield around me, O LORD; you bestow glory on me and lift up my head.
Psalm 3:3

In the morning, O LORD, you hear my voice; in the morning I lay my requests before you and wait in expectation.
Psalm 5:3

The LORD is a refuge for the oppressed, a stronghold in times of trouble.
Psalm 9:9

I love you, O LORD, my strength.
The LORD is my rock, my fortress and my deliverer; my God is my rock, in whom I take refuge. He is my shield and the horn of my salvation, my stronghold.
Psalm 18:1,2

Though an army besiege me, my heart will not fear; though war break out against me, even then will I be confident.
For in the day of trouble he will keep me safe in his dwelling; he will hide me in the shelter of his tabernacle and set me high upon a rock.
Psalm 27:3,5

My flesh and my heart may fail, but God is the strength of my heart and my portion forever.
Psalm 73:26

Praise the LORD, O my soul, and forget not all his benefits — who satisfies your desires with good things so that your youth is renewed like the eagle's.
Psalm 103:2,5

He sent forth his word and healed them; he rescued them from the grave.
Psalm 107:20

May there be peace within your walls and security within your citadels.
Psalm 122:7

In vain you rise early and stay up late, toiling for food to eat — for he grants sleep to those he loves.
Psalm 127:2

I will praise you, O LORD, with all my heart; before the "gods" I will sing your praise.
Psalm 138:1

When you lie down, you will not be afraid; when you lie down, your sleep will be sweet.
Proverbs 3:24

Wicked men are overthrown and are no more, but the house of the righteous stands firm.
Proverbs 12:7

He who fears the LORD has a secure fortress, and for his children it will be a refuge.

Proverbs 14:26

He gives strength to the weary and increases the power of the weak.

But those who hope in the LORD will renew their strength. They will soar on wings like eagles; they will run and not grow weary, they will walk and not be faint.

Isaiah 40:29,31

So do not fear, for I am with you; do not be dismayed, for I am your God. I will strengthen you and help you; I will uphold you with my righteous right hand.

Isaiah 41:10

"Not by might nor by power, but by my Spirit," says the LORD Almighty.

Zechariah 4:6b

I tell you the truth, whatever you bind on earth will be bound in heaven, and whatever you loose on earth will be loosed in heaven.

Matthew 18:18

Do not let your hearts be troubled. Trust in God; trust also in me.

Peace I leave with you; my peace I give you. I do not give to you as the world gives. Do not let your hearts be troubled and do not be afraid.

John 14:1,27

Do not be anxious about anything, but in everything, by prayer and petition, with thanksgiving, present your requests to God.

And the peace of God, which transcends all understanding, will guard your hearts and your minds in Christ Jesus.

Philippians 4:6,7

Cast all your anxiety on him because he cares for you.

1 Peter 5:7

If this is so, then the Lord knows how to rescue godly men from trials and to hold the unrighteous for the day of judgment, while continuing their punishment.

2 Peter 2:9

When You Feel Anxious

Have I not commanded you? Be strong and courageous. Do not be terrified; do not be discouraged, for the LORD your God will be with you wherever you go.

Joshua 1:9

He said: "Listen, King Jehoshaphat and all who live in Judah and Jerusalem! This is what the LORD says to you: 'Do not be afraid or discouraged because of this vast army. For the battle is not yours, but God's.'"

Early in the morning they left for the Desert of Tekoa. As they set out, Jehoshaphat stood and said, "Listen to me, Judah and people of Jerusalem! Have faith in the LORD your God and you will be upheld; have faith in his prophets and you will be successful."

2 Chronicles 20:15,20

Commit your way to the LORD; trust in him and he will do this:

He will make your righteousness shine like the dawn, the justice of your cause like the noonday sun.

Psalm 37:5,6

Trust in the LORD with all your heart and lean not on your own understanding.

Proverbs 3:5

Commit to the LORD whatever you do, and your plans will succeed.

Proverbs 16:3

Fear of man will prove to be a snare, but whoever trusts in the LORD is kept safe.

Proverbs 29:25

But blessed is the man who trusts in the LORD, whose confidence is in him.

He will be like a tree planted by the water that sends out its roots by the stream. It does not fear when heat comes; its leaves are always green. It has no worries in a year of drought and never fails to bear fruit.

Jeremiah 17:7,8

He said to her, "Daughter, your faith has healed you. Go in peace and be freed from your suffering."

Mark 5:34

"If you can?" said Jesus. "Everything is possible for him who believes."

Mark 9:23

So I say to you: Ask and it will be given to you; seek and you will find; knock and the door will be opened to you.

Luke 11:9

It will be good for those servants whose master finds them ready, even if he comes in the second or third watch of the night.

Luke 12:38

One night the Lord spoke to Paul in a vision: "Do not be afraid; keep on speaking, do not be silent.

For I am with you, and no one is going to attack and harm you, because I have many people in this city."

Acts 18:9,10

Let us then approach the throne of grace with confidence, so that we may receive mercy and find grace to help us in our time of need.

Hebrews 4:16

We do not want you to become lazy, but to imitate those who through faith and patience inherit what has been promised.

Hebrews 6:12

So do not throw away your confidence; it will be richly rewarded.

But my righteous one will live by faith. And if he shrinks back, I will not be pleased with him.

Hebrews 10:35,38

Keep your lives free from the love of money and be content with what you have, because God has said, ''Never will I leave you; never will I forsake you.''

Hebrews 13:5

Cast all your anxiety on him because he cares for you.

1 Peter 5:7

When You Face Controversy

My lips will not speak wickedness, and my tongue will utter no deceit.

Job 27:4

Since you are my rock and my fortress, for the sake of your name lead and guide me.

Free me from the trap that is set for me, for you are my refuge.

Into your hands I commit my spirit; redeem me, O LORD, the God of truth.

Psalm 31:3-5

You are my hiding place; you will protect me from trouble and surround me with songs of deliverance. Selah.

Psalm 32:7

Commit your way to the LORD; trust in him and he will do this:

He will make your righteousness shine like the dawn, the justice of your cause like the noonday sun.

Be still before the LORD and wait patiently for him; do not fret when men succeed in their ways, when they carry out their wicked schemes.

Psalm 37:5-7

I wait for you, O LORD; you will answer, O Lord my God.

Psalm 38:15

He who sacrifices thank offerings honors me, and he prepares the way so that I may show him the salvation of God.

Psalm 50:23

I call on the LORD in my distress, and he answers me.

Save me, O LORD, from lying lips and from deceitful tongues.

Psalm 120:1,2

Though I walk in the midst of trouble, you preserve my life; you stretch out your hand against the anger of my foes, with your right hand you save me.

Psalm 138:7

There are six things the LORD hates, seven that are detestable to him: haughty eyes, a lying tongue, hands that shed innocent blood, a heart that devises wicked schemes, feet that are quick to rush into evil, a false witness who pours out lies and a man who stirs up dissension among brothers.

Proverbs 6:16-19

Truthful lips endure forever, but a lying tongue lasts only a moment.

Proverbs 12:19

Commit to the LORD whatever you do, and your plans will succeed.

Proverbs 16:3

Do not say, "I'll do to him as he has done to me; I'll pay that man back for what he did."

Proverbs 24:29

When you pass through the waters, I will be with you; and when you pass through the rivers, they will not sweep over you. When you walk through the fire, you will not be burned; the flames will not set you ablaze.

Isaiah 43:2

The LORD will guide you always; he will satisfy your needs in a sun-scorched land and will strengthen your frame. You will be like a well-watered garden, like a spring whose waters never fail.

Isaiah 58:11

I the LORD search the heart and examine the mind, to reward a man according to his conduct, according to what his deeds deserve.

Jeremiah 17:10

The LORD is good, a refuge in times of trouble. He cares for those who trust in him.

Nahum 1:7

And when you stand praying, if you hold anything against anyone, forgive him, so that your Father in heaven may forgive you your sins.

Mark 11:25,26

Who is going to harm you if you are eager to do good?

1 Peter 3:13

Cast all your anxiety on him because he cares for you.

1 Peter 5:7

When You Feel Like Compromising

Be careful that you do not forget the LORD your God, failing to observe his commands, his laws and his decrees that I am giving you this day.

Deuteronomy 8:11

My son, if sinners entice you, do not give in to them.

Proverbs 1:10

Discretion will protect you, and understanding will guard you.

Proverbs 2:11

Do not set foot on the path of the wicked or walk in the way of evil men.

Avoid it, do not travel on it; turn from it and go on your way.

Proverbs 4:14,15

Stop listening to instruction, my son, and you will stray from the words of knowledge.

Proverbs 19:27

He who walks righteously and speaks what is right, who rejects gain from extortion and keeps his hand from accepting bribes, who stops his ears against plots of murder and shuts his eyes against contemplating evil — this is the man who will dwell on the heights, whose refuge will be the mountain fortress. His bread will be supplied, and water will not fail him.

Isaiah 33:15,16

The one who received the seed that fell among the thorns is the man who hears the word, but the worries of this life and the deceitfulness of wealth choke it, making it unfruitful.

Matthew 13:22

If your hand or your foot causes you to sin cut it off and throw it away. It is better for you to enter life maimed or crippled than to have two hands or two feet and be thrown into eternal fire.

Matthew 18:8

Watch and pray so that you will not fall into temptation. The spirit is willing, but the body is weak.

Matthew 26:41

Therefore do not let sin reign in your mortal body so that you obey its evil desires.

For sin shall not be your master, because you are not under law, but under grace.

Romans 6:12,14

Do not be overcome by evil, but overcome evil with good.

Romans 12:21

No temptation has seized you except what is common to man. And God is faithful; he will not let you be tempted beyond what you can bear. But when you are tempted, he will also provide a way out so that you can stand up under it.

1 Corinthians 10:13

And do not give the devil a foothold.

Ephesians 4:27

Put on the full armor of God so that you can take your stand against the devil's schemes.

Ephesians 6:11

Because he himself suffered when he was tempted, he is able to help those who are being tempted.

Hebrews 2:18

For we do not have a high priest who is unable to sympathize with our weaknesses, but we have one who has been tempted in every way, just as we are — yet was without sin.

Hebrews 4:15

No one should say, "God is tempting me." For God cannot be tempted by evil, nor does he tempt anyone.

James 1:13

When You Feel Like Lashing Out

Resentment kills a fool, and envy slays the simple.

Job 5:2

My lips will not speak wickedness, and my tongue will utter no deceit.

Job 27:4

Save me, O LORD, from lying lips and from deceitful tongues.

What will he do to you, and what more besides, O deceitful tongue?

Psalm 120:2,3

Set a guard over my mouth, O LORD; keep watch over the door of my lips.

Psalm 141:3

The mouth of the righteous is a fountain of life, but violence overwhelms the mouth of the wicked.

When words are many, sin is not absent, but he who holds his tongue is wise.

Proverbs 10:11,19

A fool shows his annoyance at once, but a prudent man overlooks an insult.

Proverbs 12:16

He who guards his lips guards his life, but he who speaks rashly will come to ruin.

Proverbs 13:3

A patient man has great understanding, but a quick-tempered man displays folly.

Proverbs 14:29

A gentle answer turns away wrath, but a harsh word stirs up anger.

Proverbs 15:1

Do not be quickly provoked in your spirit, for anger resides in the lap of fools.

Ecclesiastes 7:9

But I tell you that men will have to give account on the day of judgment for every careless word they have spoken.

For by your words you will be acquitted, and by your words you will be condemned.

Matthew 12:36,37

"In your anger do not sin": Do not let the sun go down while you are still angry.

Ephesians 4:26

But now you must rid yourselves of all such things as these: anger, rage, malice, slander, and filthy language from your lips.

Colossians 3:8

My dear brothers, take note of this: Everyone should be quick to listen, slow to speak and slow to become angry, for man's anger does not bring about the righteous life that God desires.

James 1:19,20

Likewise the tongue is a small part of the body, but it makes great boasts. Consider what a great forest is set on fire by a small spark.

James 3:5

When You Feel Threatened

After this, the word of the LORD came to Abram in a vision: "Do not be afraid, Abram. I am your shield, your very great reward."

Genesis 15:1

Blessed are you, O Israel! Who is like you, a people saved by the LORD? He is your shield and helper and your glorious sword. Your enemies will cower before you, and you will trample down their high places.

Deuteronomy 33:29

He said: "The LORD is my rock, my fortress and my deliverer."

2 Samuel 22:2

O LORD, how many are my foes! How many rise up against me!

Many are saying of me, "God will not deliver him." Selah.

But you are a shield around me, O LORD; you bestow glory on me and lift up my head.

Psalm 3:1-3

In my distress I called to the LORD; I cried to my God for help. From his temple he heard my voice; my cry came before him, into his ears.

You give me your shield of victory, and your right hand sustains me; you stoop down to make me great.

Psalm 18:6,35

The LORD is my strength and my shield; my heart trusts in him, and I am helped. My heart leaps for joy and I will give thanks to him in song.

Psalm 28:7

The angel of the LORD encamps around those who fear him, and he delivers them.

Psalm 34:7

When I am afraid, I will trust in you. In God, whose word I praise, in God I trust; I will not be afraid. What can mortal man do to me?

Psalm 56:3,4

For the LORD God is a sun and shield; the LORD bestows favor and honor; no good thing does he withhold from those whose walk is blameless.

Psalm 84:11

He will cover you with his feathers, and under his wings you will find refuge; his faithfulness will be your shield and rampart.

Psalm 91:4

You who fear him, trust in the LORD — he is their help and shield.

Psalm 115:11

You are my refuge and my shield; I have put my hope in your word.

Psalm 119:114

He is my loving God and my fortress, my stronghold and my deliverer, my shield, in whom I take refuge, who subdues peoples under me.

Psalm 144:2

So do not fear, for I am with you; do not be dismayed, for I am your God. I will strengthen you and help you; I will uphold you with my righteous right hand.

For I am the LORD, your God, who takes hold of your right hand and says to you, Do not fear; I will help you.

Isaiah 41:10,13

In addition to all this, take up the shield of faith, with which you can extinguish all the flaming arrows of the evil one.

Ephesians 6:16

When You Feel Depressed

For his anger lasts only a moment, but his favor lasts a lifetime; weeping may remain for a night, but rejoicing comes in the morning.

Psalm 30:5

But the eyes of the LORD are on those who fear him, on those whose hope is in his unfailing love.

Psalm 33:18

The righteous cry out, and the LORD hears them; he delivers them from all their troubles.

Psalm 34:17

On my bed I remember you; I think of you through the watches of the night.

Psalm 63:6

I will praise you, O LORD, with all my heart; before the ''gods'' I will sing your praise.

Psalm 138:1

He heals the brokenhearted and binds up their wounds.

Psalm 147:3

Blessed is the man who finds wisdom, the man who gains understanding.

Her ways are pleasant ways, and all her paths are peace.

She is a tree of life to those who embrace her; those who lay hold of her will be blessed.

Proverbs 3:13,17,18

The desert and the parched land will be glad; the wilderness will rejoice and blossom. Like the crocus, and the ransomed of the LORD will return.

They will enter Zion with singing; everlasting joy will crown their heads. Gladness and joy will overtake them, and sorrow and sighing will flee away.

Isaiah 35:1,10

But those who hope in the LORD will renew their strength. They will soar on wings like eagles; they will run and not grow weary, they will walk and not be faint.

Isaiah 40:31

So do not fear, for I am with you; do not be dismayed, for I am your God. I will strengthen you and help you; I will uphold you with my righteous right hand.

Isaiah 41:10

When you pass through the waters, I will be with you; and when you pass through the rivers, they will not sweep over you. When you walk through the fire, you will not be burned; the flames will not set you ablaze.

Isaiah 43:2

And provide for those who grieve in Zion — to bestow on them a crown of beauty instead of ashes, the oil of gladness instead of mourning, and a garment of praise instead of a spirit of despair. They will be called oaks of righteousness, a planting of the LORD for the display of his splendor.

Isaiah 61:3

For I am convinced that neither death nor life, neither angels nor demons, neither the present nor the future, nor any powers, neither height nor depth, nor anything else in all creation, will be able to separate us from the love of God that is in Christ Jesus our Lord.

Romans 8:38,39

Praise be to the God and Father of our Lord Jesus Christ, the Father of compassion and the God of all comfort, who comforts us in all our troubles, so that we can comfort those in any trouble with the comfort we ourselves have received from God.

2 Corinthians 1:3,4

Dear friends, do not be surprised at the painful trial you are suffering, as though something strange were happening to you.

But rejoice that you participate in the sufferings of Christ, so that you may be overjoyed when his glory is revealed.

1 Peter 4:12,13

When You Feel Lonely

The eternal God is your refuge, and underneath are the everlasting arms. He will drive out your enemy before you, saying, "Destroy him!"

Deuteronomy 33:27

For the sake of his great name the LORD will not reject his people, because the LORD was pleased to make you his own.

1 Samuel 12:22

Those who know your name will trust in you, for you, LORD, have never forsaken those who seek you.

Psalm 9:10

Even though I walk through the valley of the shadow of death, I will fear no evil, for you are with me; your rod and your staff, they comfort me.

Psalm 23:4

Though my father and mother forsake me, the
LORD will receive me.

Psalm 27:10

I was young and now I am old, yet I have never
seen the righteous forsaken or their children
begging bread.

For the LORD loves the just and will not
forsake his faithful ones. They will be protected
forever, but the offspring of the wicked will be cut
off.

Psalm 37:25,28

God is our refuge and strength, an ever-present
help in trouble.

Psalm 46:1

He heals the brokenhearted and binds up their
wounds.

Psalm 147:3

You have been a refuge for the poor, a refuge
for the needy in his distress, a shelter from the
storm and a shade from the heat. For the breath
of the ruthless is like a storm driving against a wall.

Isaiah 25:4

He gives strength to the weary and increases
the power of the weak.

Isaiah 40:29

So do not fear, for I am with you; do not be dismayed, for I am your God. I will strengthen you and help you; I will uphold you with my righteous right hand.

Isaiah 41:10

"Though the mountains be shaken and the hills be removed, yet my unfailing love for you will not be shaken nor my covenant of peace be removed," says the LORD, who has compassion on you.

Isaiah 54:10

And even the very hairs of your head are all numbered.

Matthew 10:30

And teaching them to obey everything I have commanded you. And surely I am with you always, to the very end of the age.

Matthew 28:20

Do not let your hearts be troubled. Trust in God; trust also in me.

And I will ask the Father, and he will give you another Counselor to be with you forever — the Spirit of truth. The world cannot accept him, because it neither sees him nor knows him. But you know him, for he lives with you and will be in you.

I will not leave you as orphans; I will come to you.

John 14:1,16-18

The Lord will rescue me from every evil attack and will bring me safely to his heavenly kingdom. To him be glory for ever and ever. Amen.

2 Timothy 4:18

For we do not have a high priest who is unable to sympathize with our weaknesses, but we have one who has been tempted in every way, just as we are — yet was without sin.

Let us then approach the throne of grace with confidence, so that we may receive mercy and find grace to help us in our time of need.

Hebrews 4:15,16

Keep your lives free from the love of money and be content with what you have, because God has said, "Never will I leave you; never will I forsake you."

Hebrews 13:5

Cast all your anxiety on him because he cares for you.

1 Peter 5:7

When You Feel Like Giving Up

Be strong and courageous, because you will lead these people to inherit the land I swore to their forefathers to give them.

Joshua 1:6

But the men of Israel encouraged one another and again took up their positions where they had stationed themselves the first day.

Judges 20:22

David was greatly distressed because the men were talking of stoning him; each one was bitter in spirit because of his sons and daughters. But David found strength in the LORD his God.

1 Samuel 30:6

Wait for the LORD; be strong and take heart and wait for the LORD.

Psalm 27:14

Be strong and take heart, all you who hope in the LORD.

Psalm 31:24

I wait for you, O LORD; you will answer, O Lord my God.

Psalm 38:15

But now, Lord, what do I look for? My hope is in you.

Psalm 39:7

Through you we push back our enemies; through your name we trample our foes.

Psalm 44:5

But as for me, I will always have hope; I will praise you more and more.

Psalm 71:14

Blessed is he whose help is the God of Jacob, whose hope is in the LORD his God.

Psalm 146:5

Know that the LORD is God. It is he who made us, and we are his; we are his people, the sheep of his pasture.

Psalm 100:3

I lift up my eyes to you, to you whose throne is in heaven.

As the eyes of slaves look to the hand of their master, as the eyes of a maid look to the hand of her mistress, so our eyes look to the LORD our God, till he shows us his mercy.

Psalm 123:1,2

Trust in the LORD with all your heart and lean not on your own understanding.

Proverbs 3:5

"If you can?" said Jesus. "Everything is possible for him who believes."

Immediately the boy's father exclaimed, "I do believe; help me overcome my unbelief!"

Mark 9:23,24

Therefore I tell you, whatever you ask for in prayer, believe that you have received it, and it will be yours.

Mark 11:24

But if we hope for what we do not yet have, we wait for it patiently.

Who shall separate us from the love of Christ? Shall trouble or hardship or persecution or famine or nakedness or danger or sword?

As it is written: ''For your sake we face death all day long; we are considered as sheep to be slaughtered.''

No, in all these things we are more than conquerors through him who loved us.

For I am convinced that neither death nor life, neither angels nor demons, neither the present nor the future, nor any powers, neither height nor depth, nor anything else in all creation, will be able to separate us from the love of God that is in Christ Jesus our Lord.

Romans 8:25,35,36-39

I can do everything through him who gives me strength.

Philippians 4:13

Being strengthened with all power according to his glorious might so that you may have great endurance and patience, and joyfully giving thanks to the Father, who has qualified you to share in the inheritance of the saints in the kingdom of light.

Colossians 1:11,12

Now faith is being sure of what we hope for and certain of what we do not see.

Hebrews 11:1

You, dear children, are from God and have overcome them, because the one who is in you is greater than the one who is in the world.

1 John 4:4

When You Need To Forgive

A man's wisdom gives him patience; it is to his glory to overlook an offense.

Proverbs 19:11

Do not gloat when your enemy falls; when he stumbles, do not let your heart rejoice.
Do not say, ''I'll do to him as he has done to me; I'll pay that man back for what he did.''

Proverbs 24:17,29

If your enemy is hungry, give him food to eat; if he is thirsty, give him water to drink.

Proverbs 25:21

Blessed are the merciful, for they will be shown mercy.

Matthew 5:7

But I tell you, Do not resist an evil person. If someone strikes you on the right cheek, turn to him the other also.

Matthew 5:39

But I tell you: Love your enemies and pray for those who persecute you.

Matthew 5:44

Forgive us our debts, as we also have forgiven our debtors.

For if you forgive men when they sin against you, your heavenly Father will also forgive you.

But if you do not forgive men their sins, your Father will not forgive your sins.

Matthew 6:12,14,15

Then Peter came to Jesus and asked, "Lord, how many times shall I forgive my brother when he sins against me? Up to seven times?"

Jesus answered, "I tell you, not seven times, but seventy-seven times."

Matthew 18:21,22

And when you stand praying, if you hold anything against anyone, forgive him, so that your Father in heaven may forgive you your sins.

Mark 11:25

So watch yourselves. If your brother sins, rebuke him, and if he repents, forgive him.

If he sins against you seven times in a day, and seven times comes back to you and says, "I repent," forgive him.

Luke 17:3,4

If you forgive anyone his sins, they are forgiven; if you do not forgive them, they are not forgiven.

John 20:23

Bless those who persecute you; bless and do not curse.

Do not be overcome by evil, but overcome evil with good.

Romans 12:14,21

Be kind and compassionate to one another, forgiving each other, just as in Christ God forgave you.

Ephesians 4:32

Bear with each other and forgive whatever grievances you may have against one another. Forgive as the Lord forgave you.

Colossians 3:13

Do not repay evil with evil or insult with insult, but with blessing, because to this you were called so that you may inherit a blessing.

1 Peter 3:9

When You Need Comfort

And I will ask the Father, and he will give you another Counselor to be with you forever — the Spirit of truth. The world cannot accept him, because it neither sees him nor knows him. But you know him, for he lives with you and will be in you.

I will not leave you as orphans; I will come to you.

John 14:16-18

But the Counselor, the Holy Spirit, whom the Father will send in my name, will teach you all things and will remind you of everything I have said to you.

John 14:26

But I tell you the truth: It is for your good that I am going away. Unless I go away, the Counselor will not come to you; but if I go, I will send him to you.

John 16:7

Praise be to the God and Father of our Lord Jesus Christ, the Father of compassion and the God of all comfort, who comforts us in all our troubles, so that we can comfort those in any trouble with the comfort we ourselves have received from God.

For just as the sufferings of Christ flow over into our lives, so also through Christ our comfort overflows.

2 Corinthians 1:3-5

For anyone who speaks in a tongue does not speak to men but to God. Indeed, no one understands him; he utters mysteries with his spirit.

But everyone who prophesies speaks to men for their strengthening, encouragement and comfort.

1 Corinthians 14:2,3

Therefore encourage one another and build each other up, just as in fact you are doing.

1 Thessalonians 5:11

But you, dear friends, build yourselves up in your most holy faith and pray in the Holy Spirit.

Jude 1:20

David was greatly distressed because the men were talking of stoning him; each one was bitter in spirit because of his sons and daughters. But David found strength in the LORD his God.

1 Samuel 30:6

The eternal God is your refuge, and underneath are the everlasting arms. He will drive out your enemy before you, saying, "Destroy him!"

Deuteronomy 33:27

Even though I walk through the valley of the shadow of death, I will fear no evil, for you are with me; your rod and your staff, they comfort me.

Psalm 23:4

For in the day of trouble he will keep me safe in his dwelling; he will hide me in the shelter of his tabernacle and set me high upon a rock.

Then my head will be exalted above the enemies who surround me; at his tabernacle will I sacrifice with shouts of joy; I will sing and make music to the LORD.

Psalm 27:5,6

For his anger lasts only a moment, but his favor lasts a lifetime; weeping may remain for a night, but rejoicing comes in the morning.

Psalm 30:5

I will be glad and rejoice in your love, for you saw my affliction and knew the anguish of my soul.

Psalm 31:7

Cast your cares on the LORD and he will sustain you; he will never let the righteous fall.

Psalm 55:22

Record my lament; list my tears on your scroll — are they not in your record?

Then my enemies will turn back when I call for help. By this I will know that God is for me.

In God, whose word I praise, in the LORD, whose word I praise.

Psalm 56:8-10

My comfort in my suffering is this: Your promise preserves my life.

Psalm 119:50

I remember your ancient laws, O LORD, and I find comfort in them.

Psalm 119:52

Your decrees are the theme of my song wherever I lodge.

Psalm 119:54

When You Need Encouragement

When I called, you answered me; you made me bold and stouthearted.

Psalm 138:3

Though I walk in the midst of trouble, you preserve my life; you stretch out your hand against the anger of my foes, with your right hand you save me.

The LORD will fulfill [His purpose] for me; your love, O LORD, endures forever — do not abandon the works of your hands.

Psalm 138:7,8

But you, O LORD, have mercy on me; raise me up, that I may repay them.

Psalm 41:10

When you pass through the waters, I will be with you; and when you pass through the rivers, they will not sweep over you. When you walk through the fire, you will not be burned; the flames will not set you ablaze.

Isaiah 43:2

The LORD will surely comfort Zion and will look with compassion on all her ruins; he will make her deserts like Eden, her wastelands like the garden of the LORD. Joy and gladness will be found in her, thanksgiving and the sound of singing.

Isaiah 51:3

I, even I, am he who comforts you. Who are you that you fear mortal men, the sons of men, who are but grass.

Isaiah 51:12

"For I know the plans I have for you," declares the LORD, "plans to prosper you and not to harm you, plans to give you hope and a future."

Jeremiah 29:11

May our Lord Jesus Christ himself and God our Father, who loved us and by his grace gave us eternal encouragement and good hope, encourage your hearts and strengthen you in every good deed and word.

2 Thessalonians 2:16,17

God is not unjust; he will not forget your work and the love you have shown him as you have helped his people and continue to help them.

We want each of you to show this same diligence to the very end, in order to make your hope sure.

We do not want you to become lazy, but to imitate those who through faith and patience inherit what has been promised.

Hebrews 6:10-12

But from everlasting to everlasting the LORD's love is with those who fear him, and his righteousness with their children's children.

Psalm 103:17

Be strong and courageous. Do not be afraid or terrified because of them, for the LORD your God goes with you; he will never leave you nor forsake you.

Deuteronomy 31:6

Yet I am always with you; you hold me by my right hand.

Psalm 73:23

Have I not commanded you? Be strong and courageous. Do not be terrified; do not be discouraged, for the LORD your God will be with you wherever you go.

Joshua 1:9

So he said to me, ''This is the word of the LORD to Zerubbabel: 'Not by might nor by power, but by my Spirit,' says the LORD Almighty.''

Zechariah 4:6

Trust in the LORD and do good; dwell in the land and enjoy safe pasture.

Delight yourself in the LORD and he will give you the desires of your heart.

Commit your way to the LORD; trust in him and he will do this:

He will make your righteousness shine like the dawn, the justice of your cause like the noonday sun.

Psalm 37:3-6

Praise our God, O peoples, let the sound of his praise be heard; he has preserved our lives and kept our feet from slipping.

Psalm 66:8,9

But thanks be to God, who always leads us in triumphal procession in Christ and through us spreads everywhere the fragrance of the knowledge of him.

2 Corinthians 2:14

I will praise God's name in song and glorify him with thanksgiving.

Psalm 69:30

The poor will see and be glad — you who seek God, may your hearts live!

Psalm 69:32

Being confident of this, that he who began a good work in you will carry it on to completion until the day of Christ Jesus.

Philippians 1:6

The path of the righteous is like the first gleam of dawn, shining ever brighter till the full light of day.

Proverbs 4:18

When You Need Faith

But what does it say? "The word is near you; it is in your mouth and in your heart," that is, the word of faith we are proclaiming.

Romans 10:8

Consequently, faith comes from hearing the message, and the message is heard through the word of Christ.

Romans 10:17

As for God, his way is perfect; the word of the LORD is flawless. He is a shield for all who take refuge in him.

2 Samuel 22:31

The LORD is a refuge for the oppressed, a stronghold in times of trouble.

Those who know your name will trust in you, for you, LORD, have never forsaken those who seek you.

Psalm 9:9,10

It is better to take refuge in the LORD than to trust in man.

It is better to take refuge in the LORD than to trust in princes.

Psalm 118:8,9

Those who trust in the LORD are like Mount Zion, which cannot be shaken but endures forever.

Psalm 125:1

My help comes from the LORD, the Maker of heaven and earth.

He will not let your foot slip — he who watches over you will not slumber; indeed, he who watches over Israel will neither slumber nor sleep.

Psalm 121:2-4

But let all who take refuge in you be glad; let them ever sing for joy. Spread your protection over them, that those who love your name may rejoice in you.

Psalm 5:11

May the God of hope fill you with all joy and peace as you trust in him, so that you may overflow with hope by the power of the Holy Spirit.
Romans 15:13

And we also thank God continually because, when you received the word of God, which you heard from us, you accepted it not as the word of men, but as it actually is, the word of God, which is at work in you who believe.
1 Thessalonians 2:13

But those sacrifices are an annual reminder of sins.
Hebrews 10:3

But my righteous one will live by faith. And if he shrinks back, I will not be pleased with him.
But we are not of those who shrink back and are destroyed, but of those who believe and are saved.
Hebrews 10:38,39

For everyone born of God overcomes the world. This is the victory that has overcome the world, even our faith.
1 John 5:4

The LORD himself goes before you and will be with you; he will never leave you nor forsake you. Do not be afraid; do not be discouraged.
Deuteronomy 31:8

Early in the morning they left for the Desert of Tekoa. As they set out, Jehoshaphat stood and said, "Listen to me, Judah and people of Jerusalem! Have faith in the LORD your God and you will be upheld; have faith in his prophets and you will be successful."

2 Chronicles 20:20

"Be strong and courageous. Do not be afraid or discouraged because of the king of Assyria and the vast army with him, for there is a greater power with us than with him.

With him is only the arm of flesh, but with us is the LORD our God to help us and to fight our battles." And the people gained confidence from what Hezekiah the king of Judah said.

2 Chronicles 32:7,8

Be not afraid, O land; be glad and rejoice. Surely the LORD has done great things.

Joel 2:21

See, he is puffed up; his desires are not upright — but the righteous will live by his faith.

Habakkuk 2:4

David also said to Solomon his son, "Be strong and courageous, and do the work. Do not be afraid or discouraged, for the LORD God, my God, is with you. He will not fail you or forsake you until all the work for the service of the temple of the LORD is finished."

1 Chronicles 28:20

The LORD is my shepherd, I shall not be in want.

Psalm 23:1

When You Need Healing

Surely he took up our infirmities and carried our sorrows, yet we considered him stricken by God, smitten by him, and afflicted.

But he was pierced for our transgressions, he was crushed for our iniquities; the punishment that brought us peace was upon him, and by his wounds we are healed.

Isaiah 53:4,5

When evening came, many who were demon-possessed were brought to him, and he drove out the spirits with a word and healed all the sick.

This was to fulfill what was spoken through the prophet Isaiah: "He took up our infirmities and carried our diseases."

Matthew 8:16,17

He himself bore our sins in his body on the tree, so that we might die to sins and live for righteousness; by his wounds you have been healed.

1 Peter 2:24

Christ redeemed us from the curse of the law by becoming a curse for us, for it is written: "Cursed is everyone who is hung on a tree."

Galatians 3:13

He said, "If you listen carefully to the voice of the LORD your God and do what is right in his eyes, if you pay attention to his commands and keep all his decrees, I will not bring on you any of the diseases I brought on the Egyptians, for I am the LORD, who heals you."

Exodus 15:26

Worship the LORD your God, and his blessing will be on your food and water.

I will take away sickness from among you, and none will miscarry or be barren in your land. I will give you a full life span.

Exodus 23:25,26

For the eyes of the LORD range throughout the earth to strengthen those whose hearts are fully committed to him. You have done a foolish thing, and from now on you will be at war.

2 Chronicles 16:9

Then no harm will befall you, no disaster will come near your tent.

Psalm 91:10

With long life will I satisfy him and show him my salvation.

Psalm 91:16

Praise the LORD, O my soul, and forget not all his benefits — who forgives all your sins and heals all your diseases.

Psalm 103:2,3

He sent forth his word and healed them; he rescued them from the grave.

Psalm 107:20

So is my word that goes out from my mouth: It will not return to me empty, but will accomplish what I desire and achieve the purpose for which I sent it.

Isaiah 55:11

Every good and perfect gift is from above, coming down from the Father of the heavenly lights, who does not change like shifting shadows.

James 1:17

A man with leprosy came and knelt before him and said, "Lord, if you are willing, you can make me clean."

Jesus reached out his hand and touched the man. "I am willing," he said. "Be clean!" Immediately he was cured of his leprosy.

Matthew 8:2,3

How God anointed Jesus of Nazareth with the Holy Spirit and power, and how he went around doing good and healing all who were under the power of the devil, because God was with him.

Acts 10:38

The thief comes only to steal and kill and destroy; I have come that they may have life, and have it to the full.

John 10:10

Jesus heard that they had thrown him out, and when he found him, he said, "Do you believe in the Son of Man?"

John 9:35

Jesus Christ is the same yesterday and today and forever.

Hebrews 13:8

I tell you the truth, anyone who has faith in me will do what I have been doing. He will do even greater things than these, because I am going to the Father.

John 14:12

Is any one of you sick? He should call the elders of the church to pray over him and anoint him with oil in the name of the Lord.

And the prayer offered in faith will make the sick person well; the Lord will raise him up. If he has sinned, he will be forgiven.

James 5:14,15

Dear friend, I pray that you may enjoy good health and that all may go well with you, even as your soul is getting along well.

3 John 1:2

You, dear children, are from God and have overcome them, because the one who is in you is greater than the one who is in the world.

1 John 4:4

I tell you the truth, if anyone says to this mountain, ''Go, throw yourself into the sea,'' and does not doubt in his heart but believes that what he says will happen, it will be done for him.

Therefore I tell you, whatever you ask for in prayer, believe that you have received it, and it will be yours.

Mark 11:23,24

When You Need Joy

You have made known to me the path of life; you will fill me with joy in your presence, with eternal pleasures at your right hand.

Psalm 16:11

Splendor and majesty are before him; strength and joy in his dwelling place.

1 Chronicles 16:27

And on that day they offered great sacrifices, rejoicing because God had given them great joy. The women and children also rejoiced. The sound of rejoicing in Jerusalem could be heard far away.
Nehemiah 12:43

You have filled my heart with greater joy than when their grain and new wine abound.
Psalm 4:7

I will be glad and rejoice in you; I will sing praise to your name, O Most High.
Psalm 9:2

The precepts of the LORD are right, giving joy to the heart. the commands of the LORD are radiant, giving light to the eyes.
Psalm 19:8

The LORD is my strength and my shield; my heart trusts in him, and I am helped. My heart leaps for joy and I will give thanks to him in song.
Psalm 28:7

Then my soul will rejoice in the LORD and delight in his salvation.
Psalm 35:9

Will you not revive us again, that your people may rejoice in you?
Psalm 85:6

Blessed are those who have learned to acclaim you, who walk in the light of your presence, O LORD.

They rejoice in your name all day long; they exult in your righteousness.

Psalm 89:15,16

Shout for joy to the LORD, all the earth.

Worship the LORD with gladness; come before him with joyful songs.

Psalm 100:1,2

When the LORD brought back the captives to Zion, we were like men who dreamed.

Our mouths were filled with laughter, our tongues with songs of joy. Then it was said among the nations, ''The LORD has done great things for them.''

Psalm 126:1,2

When your words came, I ate them; they were my joy and my heart's delight, for I bear your name, O LORD God Almighty.

Jeremiah 15:16

However, do not rejoice that the spirits submit to you, but rejoice that your names are written in heaven.

Luke 10:20

I have told you this so that my joy may be in you and that your joy may be complete.

John 15:11

You have made known to me the paths of life; you will fill me with joy in your presence.

Acts 2:28

And the disciples were filled with joy and with the Holy Spirit.

Acts 13:52

For the kingdom of God is not a matter of eating and drinking, but of righteousness, peace and joy in the Holy Spirit.

Romans 14:17

For you were once darkness, but now you are light in the Lord. Live as children of light.

Ephesians 5:8

Whatever you have learned or received or heard from me, or seen in me — put it into practice. And the God of peace will be with you.

Philippians 4:9

Though you have not seen him, you love him; and even though you do not see him now, you believe in him and are filled with an inexpressible and glorious joy.

1 Peter 1:8

When You Need Love

And hope does not disappoint us, because God has poured out his love into our hearts by the Holy Spirit, whom he has given us.

Romans 5:5

And this is my prayer: that your love may abound more and more in knowledge and depth of insight, so that you may be able to discern what is best and may be pure and blameless until the day of Christ, filled with the fruit of righteousness that comes through Jesus Christ — to the glory and praise of God.

Philippians 1:9-11

May the Lord make your love increase and overflow for each other and for everyone else, just as ours does for you.

May he strengthen your hearts so that you will be blameless and holy in the presence of our God and Father when our Lord Jesus comes with all his holy ones.

1 Thessalonians 3:12,13

Now about brotherly love we do not need to write to you, for you yourselves have been taught by God to love each other.

And in fact, you do love all the brothers throughout Macedonia. Yet we urge you, brothers, to do so more and more.

1 Thessalonians 4:9,10

May the Lord direct your hearts into God's love and Christ's perseverance.

2 Thessalonians 3:5

This is love: not that we loved God, but that he loved us and sent his Son as an atoning sacrifice for our sins.

Dear friends, since God so loved us, we also ought to love one another.

No one has ever seen God; but if we love one another, God lives in us and his love is made complete in us.

1 John 4:10-12

And so we know and rely on the love God has for us. God is love. Whoever lives in love lives in God, and God in him.

In this way, love is made complete among us so that we will have confidence on the day of judgment, because in this world we are like him.

There is no fear in love. But perfect love drives out fear, because fear has to do with punishment. The one who fears is not made perfect in love.

1 John 4:16-18

They want to be teachers of the law, but they do not know what they are talking about or what they so confidently affirm.

1 Timothy 1:7

Hatred stirs up dissension, but love covers over all wrongs.

Proverbs 10:12

Place me like a seal over your heart, like a seal on your arm; for love is as strong as death, its jealousy unyielding as the grave. It burns like blazing fire, like a mighty flame.

Many waters cannot quench love; rivers cannot wash it away. If one were to give all the wealth of his house for love, it would be utterly scorned.

Song of Songs 8:6,7

He who covers over an offense promotes love, but whoever repeats the matter separates close friends.

Proverbs 17:9

A friend loves at all times, and a brother is born for adversity.

Proverbs 17:17

Honor your father and mother, and love your neighbor as yourself.

Matthew 19:19

Love the LORD your God with all your heart and with all your soul and with all your strength.

Deuteronomy 6:5

And now, O Israel, what does the LORD your God ask of you but to fear the LORD your God, to walk in all his ways, to love him, to serve the LORD your God with all your heart and with all your soul.

Deuteronomy 10:12

But be very careful to keep the commandment and the law that Moses the servant of the LORD gave you: to love the LORD your God, to walk in all his ways, to obey his commands, to hold fast to him and to serve him with all your heart and all your soul.

Joshua 22:5

I love the LORD, for he heard my voice; he heard my cry for mercy.

Psalm 116:1

Jesus replied, ''I will ask you one question. Answer me, and I will tell you by what authority I am doing these things.

John's baptism — was it from heaven, or from men? Tell me!''

They discussed it among themselves and said, ''If we say, 'From heaven,' he will ask, 'Then why didn't you believe him?'

But if we say, 'From men'. . . .'' (They feared
the people, for everyone held that John really was
a prophet.)

So they answered Jesus, "We don't know."
Jesus said, "Neither will I tell you by what
authority I am doing these things."

Mark 11:29-33

A new command I give you: Love one another.
As I have loved you, so you must love one another.

All men will know that you are my disciples,
if you love one another.

John 13:34,35

Now about food sacrificed to idols: We know
that we all possess knowledge. Knowledge puffs
up, but love builds up.

1 Corinthians 8:1

The goal of this command is love, which comes
from a pure heart and a good conscience and a
sincere faith.

1 Timothy 1:5

Above all, love each other deeply, because love
covers over a multitude of sins.

1 Peter 4:8

Whoever loves his brother lives in the light, and there is nothing in him to make him stumble.
1 John 2:10

When You Need Patience

Be still before the LORD and wait patiently for him; do not fret when men succeed in their ways, when they carry out their wicked schemes.

Refrain from anger and turn from wrath; do not fret — it leads only to evil.

For evil men will be cut off, but those who hope in the LORD will inherit the land.
Psalm 37:7-9

The end of the matter is better than its beginning, and patience is better than pride.

Do not be quickly provoked in your spirit, for anger resides in the lap of fools.
Ecclesiastes 7:8,9

By standing firm you will gain life.
Luke 21:19

Not only so, but we also rejoice in our sufferings, because we know that suffering produces perserverance.

Romans 5:3

Let us not become weary in doing good, for at the proper time we will reap a harvest if we do not give up.

Galatians 6:9

As a prisoner for the Lord, then, I urge you to live a life worthy of the calling you have received.

Ephesians 4:1

Be completely humble and gentle; be patient, bearing with one another in love.

Ephesians 4:2

And we pray this in order that you may live a life worthy of the Lord and may please him in every way: bearing fruit in every good work, growing in the knowledge of God, being strengthened with all power according to his glorious might so that you may have great endurance and patience, and joyfully giving thanks to the Father, who has qualified you to share in the inheritance of the saints in the kingdom of light.

Colossians 1:10-12

And we urge you, brothers, warn those who are idle, encourage the timid, help the weak, be patient with everyone.

1 Thessalonians 5:14

May the Lord direct your hearts into God's love and Christ's perseverance.

2 Thessalonians 3:5

But you, man of God, flee from all this, and pursue righteousness, godliness, faith, love, endurance and gentleness.

1 Timothy 6:11

We do not want you to become lazy, but to imitate those who through faith and patience inherit what has been promised.

Hebrews 6:12

And so after waiting patiently, Abraham received what was promised.

Hebrews 6:15

You need to persevere so that when you have done the will of God, you will receive what he has promised.

Hebrews 10:36

Therefore, since we are surrounded by such a great cloud of witnesses, let us throw off everything that hinders and the sin that so easily entangles, and let us run with perseverance the race marked out for us.

Hebrews 12:1

Because you know that the testing of your faith develops perseverance.

Perseverance must finish its work so that you may be mature and complete, not lacking anything.

James 1:3,4

My dear brothers, take note of this: Everyone should be quick to listen, slow to speak and slow to become angry.

James 1:19

Be patient, then, brothers, until the Lord's coming. See how the farmer waits for the land to yield its valuable crop and how patient he is for the autumn and spring rains.

You too, be patient and stand firm, because the Lord's coming is near.

James 5:7,8

For this very reason, make every effort to add to your faith goodness; and to goodness, knowledge; and to knowledge, self-control; and to self-control, perseverance; and to perseverance, godliness.

2 Peter 1:5,6

This calls for patient endurance on the part of the saints who obey God's commandments and remain faithful to Jesus.

Revelation 14:12

The Lord is not slow in keeping his promise, as some understand slowness. He is patient with you, not wanting anyone to perish, but everyone to come to repentance.

2 Peter 3:9

When You Need Peace

When a man's ways are pleasing to the LORD, he makes even his enemies live at peace with him.

Proverbs 16:7

It is to a man's honor to avoid strife, but every fool is quick to quarrel.

Proverbs 20:3

Also, seek the peace and prosperity of the city to which I have carried you into exile. Pray to the LORD for it, because if it prospers, you too will prosper.

Jeremiah 29:7

Blessed are the peacemakers, for they will be called sons of God.

Matthew 5:9

Submit to God and be at peace with him; in this way prosperity will come to you.

Job 22:21

But if he remains silent, who can condemn him? If he hides his face, who can see him? Yet he is over man and nation alike.

Job 34:29

You will keep in perfect peace him whose mind is steadfast, because he trusts in you.

Trust in the LORD forever, for the LORD, the LORD, is the Rock eternal.
Isaiah 26:3,4

LORD, you establish peace for us; all that we have accomplished you have done for us.
Isaiah 26:12

Who, then, is the man that fears the LORD? He will instruct him in the way chosen for him.
He will spend his days in prosperity, and his descendants will inherit the land.
Psalm 25:12,13

Consider the blameless, observe the upright; there is a future for the man of peace.
Psalm 37:37

I will listen to what God the LORD will say; he promises peace to his people, his saints — but let them not return to folly.
Psalm 85:8

Great peace have they who love your law, and nothing can make them stumble.
Psalm 119:165

Those who trust in the LORD are like Mount Zion, which cannot be shaken but endures forever.
Psalm 125:1

To whom he said, "This is the resting place, let the weary rest"; and, "This is the place of repose" — but they would not listen.

Isaiah 28:12

"The glory of this present house will be greater than the glory of the former house," says the LORD Almighty. "And in this place I will grant peace," declares the LORD Almighty.

Haggai 2:9

My covenant was with him, a covenant of life and peace, and I gave them to him; this called for reverence and he revered me and stood in awe of my name.

Malachi 2:5

To shine on those living in darkness and in the shadow of death, to guide our feet into the path of peace.

Luke 1:79

Peace I leave with you; my peace I give you. I do not give to you as the world gives. Do not let your hearts be troubled and do not be afraid.

John 14:27

Therefore, since we have been justified through faith, we have peace with God through our Lord Jesus Christ.

Romans 5:1

For the kingdom of God is not a matter of eating and drinking, but of righteousness, peace and joy in the Holy Spirit.

Romans 14:17

Do not be anxious about anything, but in everything, by prayer and petition, with thanksgiving, present your requests to God.

And the peace of God, which transcends all understanding, will guard your hearts and your minds in Christ Jesus.

Philippians 4:6,7

Let the peace of Christ rule in your hearts, since as members of one body you were called to peace. And be thankful.

Colossians 3:15

Now may the Lord of peace himself give you peace at all times and in every way. The Lord be with all of you.

2 Thessalonians 3:16

He ransoms me unharmed from the battle waged against me, even though many oppose me.

Psalm 55:18

When You Need Protection

He who dwells in the shelter of the Most High will rest in the shadow of the Almighty.

I will say of the LORD, "He is my refuge and my fortress, my God, in whom I trust."

Surely he will save you from the fowler's snare and from the deadly pestilence.

He will cover you with his feathers, and under his wings you will find refuge; his faithfulness will be your shield and rampart.

You will not fear the terror of night, nor the arrow that flies by day, nor the pestilence that stalks in the darkness, nor the plague that destroys at midday.

A thousand may fall at your side, ten thousand at your right hand, but it will not come near you.

You will only observe with your eyes and see the punishment of the wicked.

If you make the Most High your dwelling — even the LORD, who is my refuge — then no harm will befall you, no disaster will come near your tent.

For he will command his angels concerning you to guard you in all your ways; they will lift you up in their hands, so that you will not strike your foot against a stone.

You will tread upon the lion and the cobra; you will trample the great lion and the serpent.

"Because he loves me," says the LORD, "I will rescue him; I will protect him, for he acknowledges my name.

He will call upon me, and I will answer him;
I will be with him in trouble, I will deliver him
and honor him.

With long life will I satisfy him and show him
my salvation.''

Psalm 91:1-16

Therefore let everyone who is godly pray to
you while you may be found; surely when the
mighty waters rise, they will not reach him.

You are my hiding place; you will protect me
from trouble and surround me with songs of
deliverance. Selah.

Psalm 32:6,7

''And I myself will be a wall of fire around
it,'' declares the LORD, ''and I will be its glory
within.''

Zechariah 2:5

God is our refuge and strength, an ever-present
help in trouble.

Therefore we will not fear, though the earth
give way and the mountains fall into the heart of
the sea.

Psalm 46:1,2

As for God, his way is perfect; the word of the LORD is flawless. He is a shield for all who take refuge in him.

2 Samuel 22:31

That is why I am suffering as I am. Yet I am not ashamed, because I know whom I have believed, and am convinced that he is able to guard what I have entrusted to him for that day.

2 Timothy 1:12

To him who is able to keep you from falling and to present you before his glorious presence without fault and with great joy.

Jude 1:24

When You Need Self-Control

Rather, clothe yourselves with the Lord Jesus Christ, and do not think about how to gratify the desires of the sinful nature.

Romans 13:14

For we know that our old self was crucified with him so that the body of sin might be done away with, that we should no longer be slaves to sin.

Romans 6:6

And put a knife to your throat if you are given to gluttony.

Proverbs 23:2

God is within her, she will not fall; God will help her at break of day.

Psalm 46:5

When I am afraid, I will trust in you.

In God, whose word I praise, in God I trust; I will not be afraid. What can mortal man do to me?

Psalm 56:3,4

Give us aid against the enemy, for the help of man is worthless.

With God we will gain the victory, and he will trample down our enemies.

Psalm 60:11,12

Hear my cry, O God; listen to my prayer.

From the ends of the earth I call to you, I call as my heart grows faint; lead me to the rock that is higher than I.

For you have been my refuge, a strong tower against the foe.

I long to dwell in your tent forever and take refuge in the shelter of your wings. Selah.

Psalm 61:1-4

He who fears the LORD has a secure fortress, and for his children it will be a refuge.

The fear of the LORD is a fountain of life, turning a man from the snares of death.

Proverbs 14:26,27

Better a patient man than a warrior, a man who controls his temper than one who takes a city.
Proverbs 16:32

Everything is permissible for me — but not everything is beneficial. Everything is permissible for me — but I will not be mastered by anything.
1 Corinthians 6:12

I have been crucified with Christ and I no longer live, but Christ lives in me. The life I live in the body, I live by faith in the Son of God, who loved me and gave himself for me.
Galatians 2:20

So I say, live by the Spirit, and you will not gratify the desires of the sinful nature.
Galatians 5:16

Those who belong to Christ Jesus have crucified the sinful nature with its passions and desires.
Galatians 5:24

No one serving as a soldier gets involved in civilian affairs — he wants to please his commanding officer.
2 Timothy 2:4

Dear friends, I urge you, as aliens and strangers in the world, to abstain from sinful desires, which war against your soul.
1 Peter 2:11

Therefore, since Christ suffered in his body, arm yourselves also with the same attitude, because he who has suffered in his body is done with sin.

As a result, he does not live the rest of his earthly life for evil human desires, but rather for the will of God.

1 Peter 4:1,2

If you find honey, eat just enough — too much of it, and you will vomit.

Proverbs 25:16

Everyone who competes in the games goes into strict training. They do it to get a crown that will not last; but we do it to get a crown that will last forever.

Therefore I do not run like a man running aimlessly; I do not fight like a man beating the air.

No, I beat my body and make it my slave so that after I have preached to others, I myself will not be disqualified for the prize.

1 Corinthians 9:25-27

Let your gentleness be evident to all. The Lord is near.

Philippians 4:5

When You Need Strength

The LORD is my strength and my song; he has become my salvation. He is my God, and I will praise him, my father's God, and I will exalt him.
Exodus 15:2

All his laws are before me; I have not turned away from his decrees.
2 Samuel 22:23

The LORD is my strength and my song; he has become my salvation.
Psalm 118:14

Surely God is my salvation; I will trust and not be afraid. The LORD, the LORD, is my strength and my song; he has become my salvation.
Isaiah 12:2

You armed me with strength for battle; you made my adversaries bow at my feet.
2 Samuel 22:40

It is God who arms me with strength and makes my way perfect.
Psalm 18:32

You armed me with strength for battle; you made my adversaries bow at my feet.
Psalm 18:39

May the words of my mouth and the meditation of my heart be pleasing in your sight, O LORD, my Rock and my Redeemer.

Psalm 19:14

The LORD gives strength to his people; the LORD blesses his people with peace.

Psalm 29:11

Sing for joy to God our strength; shout aloud to the God of Jacob!

Psalm 81:1

My flesh and my heart may fail, but God is the strength of my heart and my portion forever.

Psalm 73:26

A wise man has great power, and a man of knowledge increases strength.

Proverbs 24:5

Trust in the LORD forever, for the LORD, the LORD, is the Rock eternal.

Isaiah 26:4

He gives strength to the weary and increases the power of the weak.

Isaiah 40:29

But he said to me, "My grace is sufficient for you, for my power is made perfect in weakness." Therefore I will boast all the more gladly about my weaknesses, so that Christ's power may rest on me.

2 Corinthians 12:9

Summon your power, O God; show us your
strength, O God, as you have done before.
Psalm 68:28

Finally, be strong in the Lord and in his mighty
power.

Ephesians 6:10

When You Need Wisdom

I keep asking that the God of our Lord Jesus
Christ, the glorious Father, may give you the Spirit
of wisdom and revelation, so that you may know
him better.

I pray also that the eyes of your heart may be
enlightened in order that you may know the hope
to which he has called you, the riches of his
glorious inheritance in the saints, and his
incomparably great power for us who believe. That
power is like the working of his mighty strength.
Ephesians 1:17-19

For this reason, since the day we heard about
you, we have not stopped praying for you and
asking God to fill you with the knowledge of his
will through all spiritual wisdom and
understanding.

Colossians 1:9

If any of you lacks wisdom, he should ask God,
who gives generously to all without finding fault,
and it will be given to him.

But when he asks, he must believe and not doubt, because he who doubts is like a wave of the sea, blown and tossed by the wind.

That man should not think he will receive anything from the Lord; he is a double-minded man, unstable in all he does.

James 1:5-8

Such "wisdom" does not come down from heaven but is earthly, unspiritual, of the devil.

For where you have envy and selfish ambition, there you find disorder and every evil practice.

But the wisdom that comes from heaven is first of all pure; then peace-loving, considerate, submissive, full of mercy and good fruit, impartial and sincere.

Peacemakers who sow in peace raise a harvest of righteousness.

James 3:15-18

Whoever loves his brother lives in the light, and there is nothing in him to make him stumble.

But whoever hates his brother is in the darkness and walks around in the darkness; he does not know where he is going, because the darkness has blinded him.

1 John 2:10,11

Call to me and I will answer you and tell you great and unsearchable things you do not know.
Jeremiah 33:3

But you have an anointing from the Holy One, and all of you know the truth.
1 John 2:20

As for you, the anointing you received from him remains in you, and you do not need anyone to teach you. But as his anointing teaches you about all things and as that anointing is real, not counterfeit — just as it has taught you, remain in him.
1 John 2:27

Whether you turn to the right or to the left, your ears will hear a voice behind you, saying, "This is the way; walk in it."
Isaiah 30:21

Do not bring hastily to court, for what will you do in the end if your neighbor puts you to shame?
If you argue your case with a neighbor, do not betray another man's confidence.
Proverbs 25:8,9

Like an earring of gold or an ornament of fine gold is a wise man's rebuke to a listening ear.
Proverbs 25:12

I will instruct you and teach you in the way you should go; I will counsel you and watch over you.

Psalm 32:8

For with you is the fountain of life; in your light we see light.

Psalm 36:9

The unfolding of your words gives light; it gives understanding to the simple.

Psalm 119:130

If you had responded to my rebuke, I would have poured out my heart to you and made my thoughts known to you.

Proverbs 1:23

For the LORD gives wisdom, and from his mouth come knowledge and understanding.
He holds victory in store for the upright, he is a shield to those whose walk is blameless.

Proverbs 2:6,7

Send forth your light and your truth, let them guide me; let them bring me to your holy mountain, to the place where you dwell.

Psalm 43:3

Reflect on what I am saying, for the Lord will give you insight into all this.

2 Timothy 2:7

When You Need Deliverance

My soul finds rest in God alone; my salvation comes from him.

He alone is my rock and my salvation; he is my fortress, I will never be shaken.

Psalm 62:1,2

Find rest, O my soul, in God alone; my hope comes from him.

He alone is my rock and my salvation; he is my fortress, I will not be shaken.

My salvation and my honor depend on God; he is my mighty rock, my refuge.

Trust in him at all times, O people; pour out your hearts to him, for God is our refuge. Selah.

Psalm 62:5-8

One thing God has spoken, two things have I heard: that you, O God, are strong, and that you, O Lord, are loving.

Surely you will reward each person according to what he has done.

Psalm 62:11,12

If this is so, then the Lord knows how to rescue godly men from trials and to hold the unrighteous for the day of judgment, while continuing their punishment.

2 Peter 2:9

He reached down from on high and took hold of me; he drew me out of deep waters.

He rescued me from my powerful enemy, from my foes, who were too strong for me.

They confronted me in the day of my disaster, but the LORD was my support.

He brought me out into a spacious place; he rescued me because he delighted in me.

Psalm 18:16-19

In the shelter of your presence you hide them from the intrigues of men; in your dwelling you keep them safe from accusing tongues.

Psalm 31:20

I sought the LORD, and he answered me; he delivered me from all my fears.

Psalm 34:4

A righteous man may have many troubles, but the LORD delivers him from them all.

Psalm 34:19

To the Jews who had believed him, Jesus said, "If you hold to my teaching, you are really my disciples.

Then you will know the truth, and the truth will set you free."

John 8:31,32

When Jesus had called the Twelve together, he gave them power and authority to drive out all demons and to cure diseases.

Luke 9:1

He called his twelve disciples to him and gave them authority to drive out evil spirits and to heal every disease and sickness.

Matthew 10:1

I have given you authority to trample on snakes and scorpions and to overcome all the power of the enemy; nothing will harm you.

Luke 10:19

When evening came, many who were demon-possessed were brought to him, and he drove out the spirits with a word and healed all the sick.

This was to fulfill what was spoken through the prophet Isaiah: "He took up our infirmities and carried our diseases."

Matthew 8:16,17

The Lord will rescue me from every evil attack and will bring me safely to his heavenly kingdom. To him be glory for ever and ever. Amen.

2 Timothy 4:18

When You Do Not Feel God's Presence

The LORD replied, "My Presence will go with you, and I will give you rest."

Exodus 33:14

And teaching them to obey everything I have commanded you. And surely I am with you always, to the very end of the age.

Matthew 28:20

Keep your lives free from the love of money and be content with what you have, because God has said, "Never will I leave you; never will I forsake you."

Hebrews 13:5

A man of many companions may come to ruin, but there is a friend who sticks closer than a brother.

Proverbs 18:24

Greater love has no one than this, that he lay down his life for his friends.
You are my friends if you do what I command.
I no longer call you servants, because a servant does not know his master's business. Instead, I have called you friends, for everything that I learned from my Father I have made known to you.

John 15:13-15

Have I not commanded you? Be strong and courageous. Do not be terrified; do not be discouraged, for the LORD your God will be with you wherever you go.

Joshua 1:9

Because a great door for effective work has opened to me, and there are many who oppose me.

1 Corinthians 16:9

The LORD is near to all who call on him, to all who call on him in truth.

Psalm 145:18

And without faith it is impossible to please God, because anyone who comes to him must believe that he exists and that he rewards those who earnestly seek him.

Hebrews 11:6

All that the Father gives me will come to me, and whoever comes to me I will never drive away.

John 6:37

Come near to God and he will come near to you. Wash your hands, you sinners, and purify your hearts, you double-minded.

James 4:8

Here I am! I stand at the door and knock. If anyone hears my voice and opens the door, I will come in and eat with him, and he with me.

Revelation 3:20

You will seek me and find me when you seek me with all your heart.

Jeremiah 29:13

The LORD is good to those whose hope is in him, to the one who seeks him.

Lamentations 3:25

When You Have Bad Memories of the Past

Do not conform any longer to the pattern of this world, but be transformed by the renewing of your mind. Then you will be able to test and approve what God's will is — his good, pleasing and perfect will.

Romans 12:2

Therefore, if anyone is in Christ, he is a new creation; the old has gone, the new has come!

2 Corinthians 5:17

Brothers, I do not consider myself yet to have taken hold of it. But one thing I do: Forgetting what is behind and straining toward what is ahead.

Philippians 3:13

See, I am doing a new thing! Now it springs up; do you not perceive it? I am making a way in the desert and streams in the wasteland.

Isaiah 43:19

See, the former things have taken place, and new things I declare; before they spring into being I announce them to you.

Isaiah 42:9

See! the winter is past; the rains are over and gone.

Song of Songs 2:11

God presented him as a sacrifice of atonement, through faith in his blood. He did this to demonstrate his justice, because in his forbearance he had left the sins committed beforehand unpunished.

Romans 3:25

In which you used to live when you followed the ways of this world and of the ruler of the kingdom of the air, the spirit who is now at work in those who are disobedient.

All of us also lived among them at one time, gratifying the cravings of our sinful nature and following its desires and thoughts. Like the rest, we were by nature objects of wrath.

Ephesians 2:2,3

To be made new in the attitude of your minds.

Ephesians 4:23

To make her holy, cleansing her by the washing with water through the word.

Ephesians 5:26

When People Think You Are Weird

For they loved praise from men more than praise from God.

John 12:43

No, a man is a Jew if he is one inwardly; and circumcision is circumcision of the heart, by the Spirit, not by the written code. Such a man's praise is not from men, but from God.

Romans 2:29

Therefore judge nothing before the appointed time; wait till the Lord comes. He will bring to light what is hidden in darkness and will expose the motives of men's hearts. At that time each will receive his praise from God.

1 Corinthians 4:5

Peter and the other apostles replied: "We must obey God rather than men!"

Acts 5:29

If you belonged to the world, it would love you as its own. As it is, you do not belong to the world, but I have chosen you out of the world. That is why the world hates you.

John 15:19

When You Do Not Feel Like God Hears You

Moreover, I have heard the groaning of the Israelites, whom the Egyptians are enslaving, and I have remembered my covenant.

Exodus 6:5

If my people, who are called by my name, will humble themselves and pray and seek my face and turn from their wicked ways, then will I hear from heaven and will forgive their sin and will heal their land.

2 Chronicles 7:14

You will pray to him, and he will hear you, and you will fulfill your vows.

Job 22:27

Those who know your name will trust in you, for you, LORD, have never forsaken those who seek you.

Psalm 9:10

You hear, O LORD, the desire of the afflicted; you encourage them, and you listen to their cry.

Psalm 10:17

The eyes of the LORD are on the righteous and his ears are attentive to their cry.

The righteous cry out, and the LORD hears them; he delivers them from all their troubles.

Psalm 34:15,17

Evening, morning and noon I cry out in distress, and he hears my voice.

Psalm 55:17

O you who hear prayer, to you all men will come.

Psalm 65:2

Again, I tell you that if two of you on earth agree about anything you ask for, it will be done for you by my Father in heaven.

For where two or three come together in my name, there am I with them.

Matthew 18:19,20

The LORD hears the needy and does not despise his captive people.

Psalm 69:33

Hear my prayer, O LORD; listen to my cry for mercy.

Psalm 86:6

He will respond to the prayer of the destitute; he will not despise their plea.

Psalm 102:17

The LORD is near to all who call on him, to all who call on him in truth.

He fulfills the desires of those who fear him; he hears their cry and saves them.

Psalm 145:18,19

Before they call I will answer; while they are still speaking I will hear.

Isaiah 65:24

Call to me and I will answer you and tell you great and unsearchable things you do not know.

Jeremiah 33:3

This third I will bring into the fire; I will refine them like silver and test them like gold. They will call on my name and I will answer them; I will say, "They are my people," and they will say, "The LORD is our God."

Zechariah 13:9

When you pray, go into your room, close the door and pray to your Father, who is unseen. Then your Father, who sees what is done in secret, will reward you.

Do not be like them, for your Father knows what you need before you ask him.

Matthew 6:6,8

When You Want To Be Close To God

The LORD is good to those whose hope is in him, to the one who seeks him.

Lamentations 3:25

You will seek me and find me when you seek me with all your heart.

Jeremiah 29:13

Come near to God and he will come near to you. Wash your hands, you sinners, and purify your hearts, you double-minded.

James 4:8

But if from there you seek the LORD your God, you will find him if you look for him with all your heart and with all your soul.
Deuteronomy 4:29

He sought God during the days of Zechariah, who instructed him in the fear of God. As long as he sought the LORD, God gave him success.
2 Chronicles 26:5

One thing I ask of the LORD, this is what I seek: That I may dwell in the house of the LORD all the days of my life, to gaze upon the beauty of the LORD and to seek him in his temple.
For in the day of trouble he will keep me safe in his dwelling; he will hide me in the shelter of his tabernacle and set me high upon a rock.

Then my head will be exalted above the enemies who surround me; at his tabernacle will I sacrifice with shouts of joy; I will sing and make music to the LORD.
Hear my voice when I call, O LORD; be merciful to me and answer me. My heart says of you, "Seek his face!" Your face, LORD, I will seek.

Psalm 27:4-8

As the deer pants for streams of water, so my soul pants for you, O God.
My soul thirsts for God, for the living God. When can I go and meet with God?
Psalm 42:1,2

O God, you are my God, earnestly I seek you; my soul thirsts for you, my body longs for you, in a dry and weary land where there is no water.

I have seen you in the sanctuary and beheld your power and your glory.

Psalm 63:1,2

The LORD is near to all who call on him, to all who call on him in truth.

Psalm 145:18

It was not by their sword that they won the land, nor did their arm bring them victory; it was your right hand, your arm, and the light of your face, for you loved them.

Psalm 44:3

Blessed are those who hunger and thirst for righteousness, for they will be filled.

Matthew 5:6

God did this so that men would seek him and perhaps reach out for him and find him, though he is not far from each one of us.

Acts 17:27

The Spirit and the bride say, "Come!" and let him who hears say, "Come!" Whoever is thristy, let him come; and whoever wishes, let him take the free gift of the water of life.

Revelation 22:17